Science Fiction and Fantasy

Activities and Booklists for Grades 6-12

Patricia S. Morris, B.A., M.L.S.
Margaret A. Berry, B.A., M.Ed.

Volume 3

of the

Young Adult Reading Activities Library

THE CENTER FOR APPLIED RESEARCH IN EDUCATION
West Nyack, New York 10995

© 1993 by
Patricia S. Morris and Margaret A. Berry

All rights reserved.

THE CENTER FOR APPLIED
RESEARCH IN EDUCATION
Professional Publishing Division
A Division of Simon & Schuster
West Nyack, New York 10995

Permission is given for individual teachers and librarians to reproduce the student booklist pages and the student activity pages for classroom use. Reproduction of these materials for an entire school system is strictly forbidden.

The authors wish to acknowledge the following for their generous support:
The Superintendent and Board of Education of East Hanover, New Jersey.
The Staff and the Principal, Preston D. Pratola, of East Hanover Middle School.

The authors wish to acknowledge the following companies for graciously permitting inclusion of their graphics:

Kwikee InHouse Professional Art Library
Metro ImageBase, Inc.
3G Graphics, Inc. for *Images with Impact!*
Wayzata Technology Inc.
T/Maker Company for *ClickArt*

Library of Congress Cataloging-in-Publication Data

```
Morris, Patricia S.
    Young adult reading activities library / Patricia S. Morris,
Margaret A. Berry.
      p.   cm.
    "Activities and booklists for grades 6-12."
    Contents: v. 1. Modern realistic fiction -- v. 2. Historical
fiction -- v. 3. Science fiction and fantasy -- v. 4. Mystery and
suspense -- v. 5. Biography and autobiography -- v. 6. Nonfiction.
    Includes bibliographical references and indexes.
    ISBN 0-87628-585-X (v. 1)
    1. Reading (Secondary)--Language experience approach--Handbooks,
manuals, etc.   I. Berry, Margaret A.   II. Title.
LB1632.M65  1992
428.4'071'2--dc20                                           92-27620
                                                                 CIP
```

ISBN 0-87628-856-5

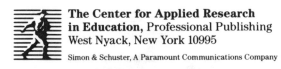

The Center for Applied Research in Education, Professional Publishing
West Nyack, New York 10995

Simon & Schuster, A Paramount Communications Company

Printed in the United States of America

ABOUT THE AUTHORS

Peg Berry, M. Ed. in Reading, is a study skills and reading teacher for the East Hanover, New Jersey, school district. Her experience includes over twenty years of teaching the middle school level, grades six, seven, and eight. She has participated in program and curriculum development on both the school and district levels. Most recently, she has presented workshops at the Educational Media Association of New Jersey, New Jersey Education Association, and New Jersey School Boards Association conventions on the role of study skills and the reading teacher in fostering a readiness for research in students. She is a 1992 recipient of the New Jersey Governor's Teacher Recognition Award.

Pat Morris, M. L. S., is a library media specialist for the East Hanover, New Jersey, school district. Her experience includes teaching self-contained classes at the elementary level, as well as high school English instruction plus over twenty years of library media experience on the elementary, middle, and high school levels. She participates regularly in program and curriculum development on both school and district levels and is currently a member of the Curriculum Research and Technology Committees for her district. A member of the Executive Board of the Educational Media Association of New Jersey, she has been a presenter and a panelist at their conventions. She has also presented at the conventions of the New Jersey School Boards Association, the New Jersey Reading Association, and the New Jersey Education Association. She received the New Jersey Governor's Teacher Recognition Award in 1989 and the Outstanding Educational Media Specialist of New Jersey Award in 1990.

About This Resource

Science Fiction and Fantasy: Activities and Booklists for Grades 6-12, Volume 3 of the *Young Adult Reading Activities Library,* (a six-volume set which also includes Modern Realistic Fiction, Historical Fiction, Mystery and Suspense, Biography, and Nonfiction) can easily supplement any existing program. The six volumes provide for the teacher or librarian:
- reproducible materials which support the whole language approach as well as resource-based instruction;
- generic activities that work with any book within the genre and encompass a range of skills, ability levels, and thinking skills; and
- booklists that include briefly annotated entries grouped by theme or subject heading, with approximate reading levels designated as easy, average, or difficult.

The booklists are comprehensive, containing new as well as old favorites likely to be found in school libraries or through interlibrary loans using a union catalog. *The Young Adult Reading Activities Library* allows easy tracking of student progress and assignments of skills and activities. Permitting the student to be an integral part of record keeping limits your administrative workload. Most importantly, reading is promoted as an important everyday activity.

In this volume you will find two booklists (one for science fiction and another for fantasy) containing themes relevant to the young adult reader. You should photocopy enough booklists so that all students will have easy access to them in either the classroom or the library. Photocopy the necessary number of "Keeping Track of Your Choices Form," or an equivalent. Review book selection and procedures with the student. You are able to choose from 26 science fiction and 26 fantasy generic worksheets when you assign activities individually, to a small group, or to an entire class. You can allow students to select their books for assignments based on their personal interests rather than at random. Given the opportunity to choose their own books, we think most students will read more. In fact, reluctant readers often get "hooked" on the joys of reading for the first time in their lives.

We would love to hear from you and your students about these activities and booklists. Send us your comments and suggestions in care of the publisher (C.A.R.E., Professional Publishing Division, 113 Sylvan Avenue, Route 9W, Englewood Cliffs, New Jersey 07632). Have fun!

Program in Six Easy Steps

1. Student selects theme and book.
2. Student copies all pertinent information on 3 x 5 form or equivalent, returns it to teacher, keeping copy for self.
3. Teacher reviews information, selects appropriate activities at convenient time.
4. Student notes activities on own copy, reads book, completes work.
5. Student hands in completed work.
6. Teacher evaluates and confers with student. Student begins selection process again.

Contents

About This Resource iv

Science Fiction and Fantasy Theme List 1

Keeping Track of Your Choices in Science Fiction and Fantasy 2

Science Fiction Booklist:
Adventure • 3   Aliens • 3   Animals • 4   Collections • 5   Communication • 6   Disasters • 6   ESP • 6   Explorers • 7   Families • 7   Games and Toys • 8   Genetics • 8   Historical Times • 9   Medicine • 9   Mystery • 9   Nonfiction • 10   Personal Conflict •10   Robotics • 11   Space Travel • 12   Space War • 12   Survival • 12   Time Travel • 14

Fantasy Booklist:
Animals • 15   Chemistry • 16   Collections • 16   Community • 17   Death and Ghosts • 18   Dragons • 19   Families • 20   Games and Toys • 21   Historical Times • 21   Kidnapping • 23   Magic • 23   Mystery • 24   Nonfiction • 24   Orphans • 24   Other Worlds • 25   Personal Conflict • 26   Robotics • 27   Royalty • 27   Supernatural • 27   Time Travel • 29   Treasure • 30   Unicorns • 30

Teacher's Notes 31

Science Fiction Activity Worksheets:

SF 1 **What Is a Science Fiction Story?** *easy* 32
Basic screen of literary elements

SF 2 **Write Yourself into the Story** *average* 33
Analysis, synthesis, written expression

SF 3 **Picture This** *easy* 34
Analysis, vocabulary development

SF 4 **Writing Dialogue** *average* 35
Analysis, change of literary format, written expression

SF 5 **Graphing Suspense** *difficult* 36
Construction of visuals, analysis, vocabulary development

SF 6 **More Time for a Minor Character** *difficult* 37
Analysis, creative written expression

SF 7 **Develop a Survey, Part I** *average* 38
Categorization, written expression

SF 8 Develop a Survey, Part II *average* 39
    Summarization, construction of graph

SF 9 Impact of Setting *difficult* 40
    Analysis, synthesis, evaluation

SF 10 Glossary *easy* 41
    Vocabulary development

SF 11 Topical Questions and Research *average* 42
    Research, written expression

SF 12 Technology *difficult* 43
    Analysis, visualization, research

SF 13 The Science in Science Fiction *difficult* 44
    Analysis, synthesis, research

SF 14 What Does Society Think? *difficult* 45
    Analysis, synthesis, evaluation, written expression

SF 15 Do Aliens Have Emotions? *easy* 46
    Analysis, written expression

SF 16 A Ticket to Ride *average* 47
    Analysis, visualization

SF 17 What Are My Rights? *difficult* 48
    Analysis, research, written expression

SF 18 Real Estate *easy* 49
    Visualization, written expression

SF 19 Transportation *average* 50
    Analysis, synthesis, evaluation, written expression

SF 20 Whether Weather *difficult* 51
    Analysis, evaluation, written expression

SF 21 Interpreting the Story *difficult* 52
    Analysis, written expression

SF 22 Author's Information *average* 53
    Research, written expression

SF 23 Dear Auntie, *average* 54
    Analysis, written expression

SF 24 **Aliens in the Kitchen** *average* 55
      Analysis

SF 25 **Progress?** *average* 56
      Analysis, written expression

SF 26 **A "Classy" Society** *average* 57
      Analysis, research, written expression

Fantasy Activity Worksheets:

FF 1 **What Is That Fantasy Book About?** *easy* 58
      Basic screen of literary elements

FF 2 **Sequence into a Cartoon** *average* 59
      Sequence of events, visualization

FF 3 **Writing a Newspaper Article** *average* 60
      Analysis, summarization

FF 4 **Bulletin Board Fantasy** *easy* 61
      Analysis, visualization, vocabulary development

FF 5 **Periodical Search** *average* 62
      Analysis of theme, research

FF 6 **Filmstrip** *average* 63
      Sequence of events, literary elements, visualization

FF 7 **Changing the Ending** *average* 64
      Original design, written expression

FF 8 **Fantasy Mobile** *easy* 65
      Vocabulary development

FF 9 **Advertising** *average* 66
      Visualization, written expression

FF 10 **Good vs. Evil** *average* 67
      Analysis, vocabulary development

FF 11 **Real vs. Unreal** *easy* 68
      Vocabulary development, literary development

FF 12 Bridging The Two Worlds *easy* 69
    Literal analysis, symbolism

FF 13 Categories of Themes *average* 70
    Literary analysis of theme

FF 14 Fantasy Symbols *difficult* 71
    Analysis, symbolism

FF 15 Changing a Symbol *difficult* 72
    Synthesis, Symbolism, visualization, creative expression

FF 16 Outlining a New Chapter *average* 73
    Creative written expression

FF 17 Outlining a Sequel *average* 74
    Literary analysis, creative written expression

FF 18 New Scene *difficult* 75
    Synthesis, creative written expression

FF 19 Character Traits *difficult* 76
    Analysis, synthesis, evaluation

FF 20 Solving Problems As a Fantastical Being *difficult* 77
    Analysis, synthesis, evaluation, point of view, creative problem solving

FF 21 The Meeting of the Beings *average* 78
    Synthesis, plot development, written expression

FF 22 What Purpose Does Fantasy Serve? *difficult* 79
    Analysis, synthesis, evaluation, personalization

FF 23 The Path of the Hero *difficult* 80
    Sequence of events, literal and literary analysis

FF 24 The Role of Clothing *easy* 81
    Analysis, evaluation

FF 25 Has It Been Used Before? *difficult* 82
    Research, symbolism, written expression

FF 26 Create Your Own Fantasy Beings *difficult* 83
    Creative written expression

Science Fiction and Fantasy Index 84

Science Fiction and Fantasy

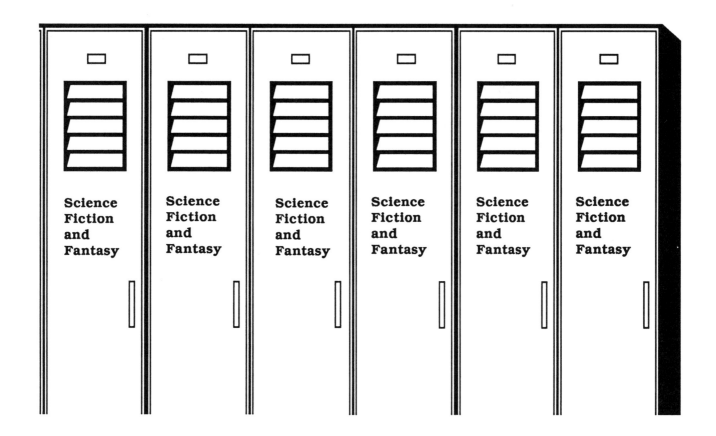

Theme List

Science Fiction

Adventure	Historical Times	
Aliens	Medicine	
Animals	Mystery	
Collection	Nonfiction	
Communication	Personal Conflict	
Disasters	Robotics	
ESP	Space Travel	
Explorers	Space War	
Families	Survival	
Games and Toys	Time Travel	
Genetics		

Fantasy

Animals	Nonfiction
Chemistry	Orphans
Collection	Other Worlds
Community	Personal Conflict
Death and Ghosts	Pirates
Dragons	Robotics
Families	Royalty
Games and Toys	Supernatural
Historical Times	Time Travel
Kidnapping	Treasure
Magic	Unicorns
Mystery	

Name_____ Section _____ Date_____

Keeping Track of Your Choices in Science Fiction/Fantasy

Fill out the two cards below for the one book that you are reading. Cut apart and give both to your teacher who will assign the appropriate activities for your book. Your teacher will then confer with you, giving you the activity sheets and your copy of the form. Complete and submit activities as instructed.

Science Fiction and Fantasy: Keeping Track of Your Choices

Student _____ Section _____
Date _____
Book Title _____
Book Author _____
Publisher _____
Copyright Date _____
Theme/Topic _____

Activities Assigned _____
Date Assigned _____
Date Submitted _____
Grade _____

Science Fiction and Fantasy: Keeping Track of Your Choices

Student _____ Section _____
Date _____
Book Title _____
Book Author _____
Publisher _____
Copyright Date _____
Theme/Topic _____

Activities Assigned _____
Date Assigned _____
Date Submitted _____
Grade _____

Science Fiction Booklist

ADVENTURE

Adams, Douglas. ***The Hitchhiker's Guide to the Galaxy.*** Pocket Books, 1979. This is a science fiction comedy about the end of the world featuring Arthur Dent and Ford Prefect, who are trying to save it. *difficult*

Daley, Brian. ***Han Solo and the Lost Legacy.*** Ballantine, 1980. A science fiction thriller in which Han Solo must outwit Xim to save himself, Chewbacca, and his Millennium Falcon. *average*

Hoover, H. M. ***The Bell Tree.*** Viking Press, 1982. Jenny and her father travel to a distant planet on vacation. While there, they find an ancient civilization and suddenly realize that they are in danger. *average*

Lucas, George. ***Star Wars.*** Ballantine, 1976. Luke Skywalker accepts the challenge of a mysterious message from an unknown princess. With courage, he finds himself and saves the galaxy. *average*

McIntyre, Vonda. ***Star Trek: The Wrath of Khan.*** Pocket Books, 1982. James Kirk is again commanding the Enterprise. This time he is to come up against an overpowering enemy, the evil Khan. If Kirk fails, the universe will be lost forever. *easy*

Mooser, Stephen. ***Space Raiders and the Planet of Doom.*** Archway, 1983. Suddenly you realize that you are commander of a rocketship entering outerspace. Your decisions while reading will determine the progress of your adventure. *average*

Pinkwater, Daniel. ***Alan Mendelsohn, the Boy from Mars.*** E. P. Dutton, 1979. Leonard's life at his new school, Bat Masterson Junior High, is just barely tolerable until he becomes friends with the unusual Alan and, with him, shares an extraordinary adventure. *difficult*

Sargent, Sarah. ***Jonas McFee, A. T. P.*** Bradbury Press, 1989. Jonas McFee is handed great power over nature by Klarinda. She and Jonas must keep the invention that created this power away from its evil inventor, her father. *easy*

Turner, Gerry. ***Stranger from the Depths.*** Scholastic, 1970. Gary and Jordan Howard are swimming when they come upon a tiny statue that resembles a lizard. Suddenly, they are thrust into the adventure of their lives as they encounter fantastic people well below the ocean floor. *average*

Wibberly, Leonard. ***Encounter near Venus.*** Farrar, Straus & Giroux, 1967. Four people try to help their friends from Nede, a satellite of Venus, overcome the evil Ka. *average*

ALIENS

Bear, Greg. ***The Forge of God.*** TOR, 1987. Three geologists find an artifact in Death Valley that they know came from nowhere on Earth. *difficult*

Bradbury, Ray. ***The Martian Chronicles.*** Bantam, 1946. Realizing that earth is at the point of destruction, a group of earthlings set out to conquer Mars. At first, it seems an easy task to accomplish. Yet as time passes, one wonders who is really conquering whom. This book is in the form of a collection of related stories. *average*

Clark, Margaret Goff. ***Barney and the UFO.*** Dodd, Mead, 1979. Barney is afraid to tell his foster parents that he has seen a UFO behind the house even when a hasty promise to Tibbo, the space boy, leads him into trouble. *easy*

Clarke, Arthur C. ***Childhood's End.*** Del Rey, 1953. Giant silver ships become part of the sky and can be seen from every major city in the world. Their

Science Fiction Booklist

mission appears to be peace. Do these aliens have another, more sinister motive? *difficult*

Clifton, Mark. ***When They Came from Space.*** Doubleday, 1962. Extraterrestials who have taken on the appearance of humans land in Washington, D. C. Ralph Kennedy knows nothing about the subject but is caught up in bureaucratic red tape. He is pressed into service and must rescue the government. *average*

Coville, Bruce. ***My Teacher Is an Alien.*** Pocket Books, 1989. Susan discovers her new substitute teacher, Mr. Smith, peeling off his face. Is anyone going to believe an alien is among them? *average*

DeWeese, Gene. ***Nightmares from Space.*** Franklin Watts, 1981. Some teenagers have an encounter with an alien which leaves them with special mental powers. *easy*

Harding, Lee. ***The Fallen Spaceman.*** Bantam, 1973. One small alien, Tyro, is tucked inside a huge space suit working outside the spaceship, which suddenly departs without him. Erik sees him fall to Earth and crawls inside the suit to find that he and Tyro are both trapped. *easy*

Hogan, James P. ***Code of the Lifemaker.*** Ballantine, 1983. Robots living on Titan have evolved a civilization with culture, religion, and politics. A human interplanetary probe finds them. Will their civilization vanish? *difficult*

Jones, Diana Wynn. ***Dogsbody.*** Greenwillow, 1977. Sirius, the Dog Star, is banished from the sky because he allows an item to fall to Earth. Unfortunately, when he comes to Earth, he is a dog and becomes the friend of a lovely young girl. *average*

Land, Charles. ***Calling Earth.*** Creative Education, 1978. Amad says that he is an inhabitant of the Twenty-First Galaxy and is in need of help. John and Vic set out to help this unknown force, putting themselves in a great deal of danger. *easy*

Lawrence, Louise. ***Moonwind.*** Harper & Row, 1986. Gareth wins an essay competition and his prize is a trip to the moon. There he meet and falls in love with Bethkahn who is stranded there in her crippled spaceship. But Bethkahn is 10,000 years old. *average*

Ray, N. L. ***There Was this Man Running.*** Macmillan, 1981. The family of a storekeeper becomes involved with a mysterious alien menace. *average*

Service, Pamela F. ***Under Alien Stars.*** Atheneum, 1990. The powerful Tsorians, having defeated the inhabitants of Earth through powerful weapons and technology, suddenly find they must band with a group called the Earth's Resisters to fight another even more powerful force. *average*

Wells, H. G. ***The War of the Worlds.*** *any edition*. Martians armed with death rays invade the Earth. *average*

ANIMALS

Bell, Clare. ***Ratha's Creature.*** Margaret K. McElderry, 1983. Ratha, a superior-intelligence cat, learns to use fire. She saves another clan even though she is in exile. *difficult*

Bell, Clare. ***Tomorrow's Sphinx.*** Macmillan, 1986. This unusual story of two black cheetahs who share a mental link also leaps back in time to Ancient Egypt. *difficult*

Crichton, Michael. ***Jurassic Park.*** Alfred A. Knopf, 1990. Would you be willing to visit the newest in theme parks and see live dinosaurs on a remote island? What if the dinosaurs escaped? *average*

Science Fiction Booklist

Harrison, Harry. ***The Man from P.I.G. and R.O.B.O.T.*** Atheneum, 1979. Humorous accounts of specially trained and bred pigs of the Robot Obtrusion Batallion give eleven thousand new space policeman insight into possible assignments. *average*

Norton, Andre. ***Breed to Come.*** Viking, 1972. Furtig, a young warrior who happens to be a cat, finds that Demons, those animals called humans, might return to this planet, the planet they poisoned. The poison, only destructive to humankind, helps Furtig's race thrive. *average*

Norton, Andre. ***Moon of Three Rings.*** Viking Press, 1966. Maelen and her strange pet barsks live on the planet Yiktor. Krip is drawn to help her fight the evil powers. *difficult*

Norton, Andre. ***Star Ka'at.*** Pocket Books, 1976. Two cats with very special powers come to Earth on an important mission to rescue someone in trouble. *easy*

Sanders, Scott Russell. ***The Engineer of Beasts.*** Franklin Watts, 1988. Mooch, a thirteen-year-old orphan, lives in a domed floating city in the future. She hires on to help Orlando Spinks run the New Boston Disney, but she still needs to understand the wild animals outside the city. *average*

COLLECTIONS

Star Trek: The New Voyages. Bantam, 1978. This collection contains some of the best short stories written by fans of Star Trek. *average*

Asimov, Isaac. ***Asimov's Mysteries.*** Doubleday, 1968. A wonderful collection of stories by the noted master includes the story "The Dying Night." *average*

Asimov, Isaac. ***The Foundation Trilogy.*** Doubleday, 1987. This book includes *Foundation*, *Foundation and Empire* and *Second Foundation*. It also includes the famous *I, Robot*. *difficult*

Asimov, Isaac, ed. ***Tomorrow's Children.*** Doubleday, 1966. This collection of eighteen tales of fantasy and science fiction by noted authors includes Ray Bradbury's *All Summer in a Day* in which one day of summer sunshine occurs once every seven years on another planet. *average*

Conklin, Groff, ed. ***The Omnibus of Science Fiction.*** Bonanza Books, 1980. This is a collection of forty-two classic works of science fiction short stories. *difficult*

Engdahl, Sylvia. ***Anywhere, Anywhen: Stories of Tomorrow.*** Atheneum, 1976. This collection of five stories of a future somewhere, sometime includes "The Left-Handed Boy." What happens if you are the son of the Manager of Interplanetary Finance and you do not fit the government's perception of what is acceptable in conduct and education? Is a Personality Alteration the only avenue left? *average*

Ginsburg, Mirra, ed. ***The Air of Mars.*** Macmillan, 1976. Nine Soviet stories of science fiction and fantasy, edited and translated by Mirra Ginsburg. *average*

Green, Roger Lancelyn, ed. ***Thirteen Uncanny Tales.*** E. P. Dutton, 1970. The stories include "The Bottle Imp" by Robert Louis Stevenson and "Farms of Things Unknown" by C. S. Lewis. *average*

Greenberg, Martin H., ed. ***101 Science Fiction Stories.*** Avenel Books, 1986. This collection of stories includes 101 short stories from 86 different authors. *average*

Science Fiction Booklist

Harrison, Harry, ed. *Nova 4.* Walker, 1974. Thirteen short stories are included in this collection. *average*

Knight, Damon, ed. *Orbit 9.* G. P. Putnam's Sons, 1971. Some of the stories in this collection deal with mind experiments. *average*

Santesson, Hans Stefan, ed. *The Days after Tomorrow.* Little, Brown & Co., 1971. Thought-controlling teddy bears, archaeological digs on Mars, and weather control are some of the topics of interest in this collection. *average*

Silverberg, Robert, ed. *Great Tales of Science Fiction.* Castle, 1985. This is a collection of science fiction short stories that provide an overview of what has been written from the mid-nineteenth century up to today. *difficult*

COMMUNICATION

Clarke, Arthur C. *Dolphin Island.* Holt, Rinehart & Winston, 1963. The dolphins, the "people" of the sea, help the humans when danger appears. *average*

Dunbar, Robert E. *Into Jupiter's World.* Franklin Watts, 1981. Strange radio signals alert the authorities at Space Station Mars that something is wrong on Jupiter. Four young cadets set out from Mars with Captain Milo as captain of a team, led by Will Pachek, to correct the problem. *easy*

Yep, Laurence. *Sweetwater.* Harper & Row, 1973. Amadeus has taught students to sing on the planet Harmony. Suddenly, his abilities bring fear into the hearts of the family of one of his students, fear of the seadragon and the flood. *average*

DISASTERS

Clarke, Arthur C. *A Fall of Moondust.* Harcourt Brace Jovanovich, 1961. The Moon is a popular vacation spot. An accident occurs and a ship carrying a crew and passengers on vacation are buried beneath fifteen meters of moondust. The resulting rescue operation is riveting. *difficult*

Dickinson, Peter. *Heartsease.* Little, Brown & Co., 1969. The Changes come to Great Britain and rule that anyone guilty of using a machine shall be condemned as a witch. *average*

Wiessner, John. *Space Bugs: Earth Invasion.* Torrance & Company, 1983. It is the year 1982, in New Jersey, that Garrison and Morgan realize that the President has disappeared and has been replaced by an insect-like creature, Queen Termita. With special knowledge, they set out to save the country. *average*

ESP

Bethancourt, T. Ernesto. *Instruments of Darkness.* Holiday House, 1979. A companion novel to *The Mortal Instruments*, this book concerns some strange events and a plot to control the world. *average*

Bethancourt, T. Ernesto. *The Mortal Instruments.* Holiday House, 1977. An inner-city Hispanic teenager develops an ESP ability which becomes a monstrous threat to civilization. *average*

Bova, Benjamin. *The Dueling Machine.* Holt, Rinehart, & Winston, 1969. The dueling machine is used to keep peace throughout the universe in the future. Everything works well until an earthbound power decides how to

Science Fiction Booklist

control the machine in order to control the rest of the universe. *average*

Nourse, Alan E. **Psi High and Others**. McKay, 1967. Will Earth pass the test to become part of the Galactic Confederation or will they no longer be worth anything? *average*

Sutton, Jean. **Lord of the Stars**. G. P. Putnam, 1969. Gultur, Lord of the Stars, would like to conquer the universe. The likelihood that he can do this is pretty good considering that he has eight arms. However, a young earthling challenges him to duel using ESP. *average*

Vinge, Joan. **Psion**. Dell, 1982. Cat, sixteen, is an orphan from the slums. His parentage is mixed: alien and human, which might explain his psionic talents. *difficult*

Walters, Hugh. **Mission to Mercury**. Criterion Books, 1965. Chris Godfrey and his friends resent having a female added to the space crew. She helps rescue the mission because she has ESP with her twin sister back on Earth. *average*

EXPLORERS

Benford, Gregory and David Brin. **Heart of the Comet**. Bantam, 1986. Did you ever wonder what it would be like to colonize Halley's Comet? *difficult*

Crichton, Michael. **Sphere**. Alfred A. Knopf, 1987. In a thousand feet of water, experts try to find out the secrets of the large spaceship they found there. *difficult*

Del Rey, Lester. **Moon of Mutiny.** Holt, Rinehart, & Winston, 1961. Fred Halpern disobeys orders and is expelled from the Space Academy. He is given another chance to join an expedition. Will he disobey orders again? *average*

Heinlein, Robert A. **Rocket Ship Galileo.** Ballantine, 1974. A drama of exploration and discovery that tells the story of four young men who formed the Galileo Club in the hopes of landing their own amateur rocket on the moon. Successfully launched, it seems that space is not their only enemy. *average*

Hoover, H. M. **Another Heaven, Another Earth.** Viking Press, 1981. A small community of humans has regressed to a primitive agricultural society. But an exploratory seach comes from space to their far distant planet to find new worlds for human habitation. What will happen to them? *difficult*

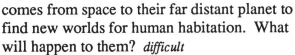

Karl, Jean E. **But We Are Not of the Earth.** E.P. Dutton, 1981. Four students from Meniscus delight in the habitable but unihabited planet they discover until they realize that all is not as it seems. *average*

McIntyre, Vonda. **Starfarers**. Ace Books, 1989. The Starfarer plans to begin a search for intelligent life in the universe. The crew will be commanded by Victoria MacKenzie. This will be America's second attempt. The first ship and crew were lost in space. *difficult*

FAMILIES

Blackwood, Gary. **The Dying Sun**. Atheneum, 1989. Set in the middle of the twenty-first century, during a new ice age, James must leave his home in the violent yet warmer area of the

Science Fiction Booklist

United States to join his parents in the less-populated colder region. James soon finds that both ways of life are a dangerous choice for different reasons. *average*

Fisk, Nicholas. ***A Rag, a Bone, and a Hank of Hair.*** Crown Publishers, 1982. It is the twenty-third century. Children are not plentiful, but one very bright boy is being sent to live with a London family. Why? *easy*

Gilden, Mel. ***Outer Space and All that Junk.*** Lippincott, 1989. Myron's Uncle Hugo is a little weird. He collects junk and claims that it is really stranded aliens. Furthermore, he has a plan to get them back home. What is Myron to do? *average*

Mahy, Margaret. ***Aliens in the Family.*** Scholastic, 1985. Jake Raven, expecting to dislike his new stepsister and stepbrother, ends up helping them protect an alien from another dimension as he flees from mysterious pursuers with the ability to alter time. *average*

Voight, Cynthia. ***Building Blocks.*** Atheneum, 1984. In a trip back in time, Brann meets his father as a ten-year-old and learns for the first time to love and understand him. *difficult*

GAMES AND TOYS

Card, Orson Scott. ***Ender's Game.*** TOR, 1985. The game that Ender Wiggins plays extremely well, even though he is only six, is war. For that ability he is chosen to lead Earth to victory in a galactic war. *difficult*

Hughes, Monica. ***Invitation to the Game.*** Simon & Schuster, 1990. Benta and Lissie are graduating but must live in an old abandoned warehouse because there are no jobs available. But then they get involved in The Game, an innocent pasttime. Suddenly, their own survival is at stake. *average*

Sleator, William. ***Interstellar Pig.*** Bantam, 1984. Barney is bored at the summer beach cottage. When he investigates his weird neighbors and their unusual board game, he becomes Earth's representative against bizarre aliens. *average*

GENETICS

Alcock, Vivien. ***The Monster Garden.*** Delacorte, 1988. Frankie Stein's brother, David, takes a lab sample from his father's work experiments. Through her own efforts, Frankie creates Monnie, a fast-growing creature who becomes a friend. *average*

Forrester, John. ***Bestiary Mountain.*** Bradbury Press, 1985. Old Earth has been the battleground for a genetic war. Four teenagers must come back to help right a wrong. But the four are not all human: there is at least one scientifically created person. *average*

Sleator, William. ***The Duplicate.*** E. P. Dutton, 1988. Sixteen-year-old David, finding a strange machine that creates replicas of living organisms, duplicates himself and suffers the horrible consequence of having the duplicate turn against him. *average*

Yep, Laurence. ***Monster Makers, Inc.*** Penguin Books, 1986. Rob helps rescue his father, a famous geneticist, who has been kidnapped. His dad has made some lovely prehistoric pets, including a four foot Godzilla. *difficult*

Science Fiction Booklist

HISTORICAL TIMES

Anderson, Poul. ***A Midsummer Tempest.*** Doubleday, 1974. Rupert, Prince of the Rhine, escapes from his captives the Roundheads. Shakespeare appears as an historian. *difficult*

Asimov, Janet and Isaac. ***Norby and Yobo's Great Adventure.*** Walker & Co., 1989. When Jeff and his robot, Norby, accompany Admiral Yobo to prehistoric times so the admiral can do family research, the trip turns into a dangerous mission. *easy*

Hughes, Monica. ***The Guardian of Isis.*** Atheneum, 1981. No more technical knowledge exists for the settlers on Isis. They are dominated by an absolute ruler and have reverted to a primitive society. This book is a sequel to *The Keeper of the Isis Light*. *average*

Ormondroyd, Edward. ***Time at the Top.*** Bantam, 1963. Upon entering her apartment building, Susan, upset by the day's events, steps into the elevator to get to her home. She does not arrive there. Instead, she finds herself swept back in time, living with a family in the mid-1800's. There is no promise of ever returning. *average*

MEDICINE

Asimov, Isaac. ***Fantastic Voyage.*** Doubleday, 1987. A medical team is miniaturized and injected into a body. A thriller and a chiller... no human brain has ever been used this way. *difficult*

Bonham, Frank. ***The Forever Formula.*** E. P. Dutton, 1979. Seventeen-year-old Evan Clark wakes up in a hospital bed so cold that he can see the frost on his hands. Then he sees the nurses, who are clones of each other, and he spots "Iron Eyes" outside his door. Iron Eyes stares at him through large, rotating metal orbs instead of eyes. *average*

Dickinson, Peter. ***Eva.*** Del Rey, 1989. Eva wakes up in a hospital. She finds out that doctors have saved her life by transferring her neuron memory into the brain of a female chimpanzee. *difficult*

Keyes, Daniel. ***Charly.*** Bantam, 1966. An operation is used as a laboratory experiment to increase Charlie Gordeon's intelligence. The book traces Charlie's struggle toward intelligence only to find out that experiments are not always successful. *average*

Lightner, A. M. ***Doctor to the Galaxy.*** W. W. Norton, 1965. When Dr. Garrison Bart completes his medical studies on earth, he finds a position on the planet Acoma. Unfortunately, what Acoma needs is a veterinarian. *average*

Webb, Sharon. ***Earthchild.*** Macmillan, 1982. A medical treatment, recently discovered, makes children immortal. It does not do that to adults, who become violently jealous. *difficult*

MYSTERY

Adams, Douglas. ***Dirk Gently's Holistic Detective Agency.*** Simon & Schuster, 1987. A detective meets a bewildered ghost, a cellist, a computer fanatic, and a time traveler on his search for the origin of life on Earth. *difficult*

Bonham, Frank. ***The Missing Persons League.*** Scholastic, 1976. What has happened to some people? Is anyone going to try to find them? *easy*

Carlsen, Ruth Christopher. ***Ride a Wild Horse.*** Houghton Mifflin, 1970. When Julie comes to live with the Sutton family, a mystery begins and twelve-year-old Barney is in for some bewildering experiences. *average*

Carlson, Dale. ***The Plant People.*** Franklin Watts, 1977. A mysterious fog which settles over the town changes almost everyone into a plant. *easy*

Science Fiction Booklist

Dickson, Gordon R. *Secret under the Caribbean.* Holt, Rinehart, 1964. Robby Hoenig, curious about the value of an excavation of an eighteenth century sloop, joins the team. *average*

Slote, Alfred. *The Trouble on Janus.* Lippincott, 1985. Jack and his robot buddy, Danny One, set off to the planet Janus. They must rescue the young King Paul from his conniving uncle. *average*

NONFICTION

Bova, Ben. *Notes to a Science Fiction Writer.* Charles Scribner's Sons, 1974. Would you like to be able to write a science fiction novel as well as read one? This book discusses the craft of writing science fiction in terms of characters, background, conflict, and plot. *average*

Dozois, Gardner. *Writing Science Fiction and Fantasy.* St. Martin's Press, 1991. This collection of essays from experts in the field cover all aspects of writing for this particular market, including suggestions for further reading. *average*

Merriam, Eve. *Ab to Zogg: A Lexicon for Science Fiction and Fantasy Readers.* Atheneum, 1977. This is a lexicon, or glossary, of invented words and phrases often found in fantasy and science fiction. With tongue in cheek, each entry provides the reader with a word game of puns, plays on words, and unlikely allusions. *easy*

Nicholls, Peter. *The Science in Science Fiction.* Crescent, 1982. This book offers an analysis of the scientific concepts and phenomena reported as realities in science fiction. It indicates which are really rooted in the possible, which are already operational, and which are impossible as we know technology today. *difficult*

Weaver, Tom. *Science Fiction Stars and Horror Heroes.* McFarland, 1991. This is a compilation of interviews with actors, directors, producers, and writers from the 1940's through the 1960's woven together to produce a fascinating account the development of the field. *average*

PERSONAL CONFLICT

Arnason, Eleanor. *A Woman of the Iron People.* Morrow, 1991. What is her role in life? *difficult*

Bradbury, Ray. *Fahrenheit 451.* Ballantine, 1953. Guy Montag believes that books should be destroyed as they are a threat to society. Fahrenheit 451 is the temperature at which books burn. One day as he discovers his grave mistake, he also realizes that he is doomed. His only hope is to run. *average*

Christopher, John. *Wild Jack.* Macmillan, 1974. This is a science fiction drama, set in twenty-third century England, concerning Clive Anderson's struggle against mind control and his search for personal freedom. *difficult*

Dereske, Jo. *The Lone Sentinel.* Atheneum, 1989. Erik's father suffers a fatal accident which leaves Erik tending the strange crop, biosote, on a distant Earth colony. This crop is sold to the alien Helgatites. *average*

Heinlein, Robert A. *A Stranger in a Strange Land.* Berkley, 1961. Valentine Michael Smith has arrived from Mars. He has superhuman abilities but still has difficulty understanding the everyday customs and traditions of his new neighbors on planet Earth. *difficult*

L'Engle, Madeline. *A Ring of Endless Light.* Farrar, Straus & Giroux, 1980. Vicky Austin confronts questions of love and death and of dependence and responsibility. *easy*

© 1993 Patricia S. Morris and Margaret A. Berry

Science Fiction Booklist

McKillip, Patricia A. ***Fool's Run.*** Watner, 1987. The Queen of Hearts is part of a band coming to entertain the convicts at an orbiting prison. In the prison is another woman convicted when she was 21 of murdering 1,509 innocent people. Do the two have something in common? *average*

Silverberg, Robert. ***Thorns.*** Bantam, 1967. Minner Burris, Lona Kelvin, and Duncan Chalk are caught in the emotions of their situations and what each has become, a misfit in society. Somehow they do not even fit together as a threesome. *difficult*

Townsend, John. ***Noah's Castle.*** Lippincott, 1975. Personal conflicts and societal problems are studied as this drama questions one family's struggle to survive in a world gone out of control. Can they stockpile enough and stay alive? *average*

ROBOTICS

Asimov, Isaac. ***Foundation and Earth.*** Doubleday, 1986. Golan Trevize searches for the lost planet Earth in the hopes of finding a key to develop a new organism that will be common to all thinking beings. This is fifth in the Foundation series. *difficult*

Beatty, Jerome. ***Maria Looney and the Remarkable Robot.*** Avon, 1979. Tommy Tonn, a robot who works for the Looney family doing all their household chores, is robotnapped. *easy*

Beatty, Jerome. ***Matthew Looney's Voyage to the Earth.*** Avon, 1972. On the way to Planet Freeholy, where he plans to establish a colony, Matthew Looney meets space pirates who force him into oblivion. While floating, he encounters an expedition that rescues him. This is just the beginning of his adventure. *easy*

Benford, Gregory. ***Against Infinity.*** Pocket Books, 1983. Ganymede, Jupiter's moon, is where animals from Earth go to be refitted with robotic parts and given a minimal intelligence. *difficult*

Caidin, Martin. ***Cyborg.*** Warner Books, 1972. Lt. Col. Steve Austin (The Bionic Man) must learn to cope with being part human and part super-powered mechanical man. Somehow he feels through the accident and the recreation of his person that he has lost a large part of himself, his emotions. *difficult*

Clement, Hal. ***Still River.*** Ballantine, 1987. Five graduate students in science are sent to study a very small planet, Enigma. Four of the students are not human. *difficult*

Heinlein, Robert A. ***Friday.*** Ballantine, 1982. Friday is a female who works in a very dangerous military job. She is also a nonhuman who looks very much like a female human movie star. But this bionic wonder wants to belong to the human race. *difficult*

McMahan, Ian. ***The Fox's Lair.*** Macmillan, 1983. Karen's father, Mr. Fujisawa, has been blamed for a computer malfunction which has resulted in a five million dollar shortfall. Ricky, with the help of an electronic computer personality, sets out to track the real thieves. *easy*

Slote, Alfred. ***Omega Station.*** Lippincott, 1983. Jack Jameson has a robot twin, Danny One. They must save the universe. *easy*

Wilkes, Marilyn Z. ***C.L.U.T.Z. and the Fizzion Formula.*** Dial, 1985. Imprisoned in a basement as spies, Rodney Pentax, his dog, Aurora, and his guardian robot, Clutz, were planning to escape. Suddenly, they realized that the formula over which they were held hostage must be more important than just the recipe for the contents of a can of soda. *easy*

Science Fiction Booklist

SPACE TRAVEL

Caldwell, Steven. *The Fantastic Planet.* Crescent, 1980. It is the responsibility of Galactic Federation to protect its membership yet provide leadership in extending knowledge and understanding of the world outside. It is through the efforts of the Galactic Research Institute that most missions begin. This is how the crew of the Stellar Ranger becomes involved in an extraordinary and dangerous adventure. *average*

Cameron, Eleanor. *Stowaway to the Mushroom Planet.* Little, Brown & Co., 1956. Chuck and David are cautioned by Mr. Tycho Bass not to reveal their knowledge of Basidium, the Mushroom Planet. All is well until the next trip, when Horatio Q. Peabody stows away. *easy*

Clarke, Arthur C. *2001: A Space Odyssey.* New American Library, 1968. HAL is the computer who interfaces with the crew. Is HAL only a computer or is he more? And what is he up to? *average*

Heinlein, Robert A. *Citizen of the Galaxy.* Charles Scribner's Sons, 1957. Thorby travels from planet to planet searching for clues to unlock his own past. *difficult*

Lesser, Milton. *Stadium beyond the Stars.* Holt, Rinehart, & Winston, 1960. Steve Frazer is on his way to compete in the Interstellar Olympic Games. Is the spaceship he sights and investigates going to keep him from participating in the Olympics? *average*

Slote, Alfred. *My Trip to Alpha I.* Lippincott, 1978. VOYA-CODE is the most sophisticated form of interplanetary travel, but a young boy, Jack, finds it is not without danger. *easy*

Tubb, E. C. *Space: 1999-Alien Seed.* Pocket Books, 1976. During an intergalactic flight, the men and women of Moonbase Alpha encounter innocent-looking pods, unearthed from old space dust. This is to become either a life force to be returned to the Moonbase or their worst nightmare. *average*

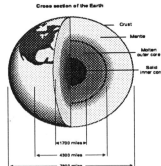

Verne, Jules. *A Journey to the Center of the Earth.* any edition. Travel with Professor Hardwigg, his nephew, and Hans through an active volcano to the center of the earth. *average*

SPACE WAR

Bear, Greg. *Eon.* St. Martin's Press, 1985. Civilization on Earth is on the brink of being history forever. Suddenly, the Stone appears. Is it a spaceship? Is it an asteroid? Will it save Earth from destruction? *difficult*

Bujold, Louis McMaster. *The Warrior's Apprentice.* Simon & Schuster, 1986. Miles Vorkosigan is only seventeen so he masquerades as a space warrior. In a short while, he finds himself commanding 3,000 troops and nineteen warships. *difficult*

Caldwell, Steven. *Star Quest.* Crescent, 1979. It is the Federation's responsibility to protect its satellite colonies. When it becomes aware that an alien force has broken through its perimeter, courageous volunteers set out on a mission that will change the course of their lives, forever. *easy*

Hill, Douglas. *Galactic Warlord.* Margaret K. McElderry, 1980. Keill Randor will stop at nothing to save his home and his home world. He even becomes bionic. *average*

SURVIVAL

Bachman, Richard. *The Long Walk.* Signet, 1979. The sports event is a 450-mile marathon

Science Fiction Booklist

walk. Garraty Raymond Davis is to be one of the a hundred competitors. The top prize is great fortune and fame, but most contestants die before reaching the finish line and no one will ever know what happened. (Richard Bachman is a pen name of Stephen King.) *difficult*

Christopher, John. ***The White Mountains.*** Macmillan, 1967. Will and Jean-Paul, or Bean-Pole as he is known to his friends, want to escape being "capped" by the conquering Tripods as their friends have been. How will they manage? This is the first book in a trilogy; *City of Gold and Lead* and *Pool of Fire* are the others. *easy*

Engdahl, Sylvia. ***Enchantress from the Stars.*** Atheneum, 1970. Elena is a stowaway on board her father's spaceship going to one of three different civilizations from three different planets which clash. Will the encounter be good or disastrous? What will Elena's part be? *difficult*

Frank, Pat. ***Alas, Babylon.*** Bantam, 1979. A community struggles to survive after a nuclear war isolates them and presents many day-to-day challenges. *difficult*

Heinlein, Robert A. ***Farmer in the Sky.*** Ballantine, 1972. George Lerner does not want his son, Bill, to join him aboard the ship, *The Mayflower*, which is shipping out to the new colony, Ganymede. He feels that the mission is just too hazardous. Bill manages to join the crew and finds danger at every turn. *average*

Johnson, Annabel and Edgar. ***A Memory of Dragons.*** Atheneum, 1986. Paul Killian is only eighteen, but is considered a genius in creating technical tools. This story is set in the future at a time when the natural resources in the United States are almost depleted. He is caught between two factions. One side wants the U. S. to stay united and the other side wants the western states to secede from the Union. *average*

Kelley, Leo P. ***Star Gold.*** Fearon, 1979. Brett Kinkaid has been sentenced to the prison planet, Earth, for killing a man. Suddenly he finds a way to escape but will it be worth the price he has to pay for freedom? *easy*

Lawrence, Louise. ***Children of the Dust.*** Harper & Row, 1985. Catherine is the middle generation in this story of nuclear devastation. She survives in a sealed room, and her father survives in an underground bunker. The generation that comes after them evolves as a new species in order to cope. *average*

Nelson, O. T. ***The Girl Who Owned a City.*** Dell, 1975. Lisa is determined to lead all to a better life. An unexpected virus has killed all humans over the age of twelve, and America is in total disorder. *average*

O'Brien, Robert C. ***Z for Zachariah.*** Dell, 1974. Ann Burden thinks that she is the only survivor of a nuclear bomb until she spots smoke in the distance. As a being approaches, she begins to fear for her life. *average*

Palmer, David R. ***Emergence.*** Bantam, 1984. Candy Smith-Foster survives a bionuclear war and lives to tell her story in phrases written in her journal. She searches Earth for other survivors. *difficult*

Paton Walsh, Jill. ***The Green Book.*** Farrar, Straus & Giroux, 1982. Refugees from Earth struggle to survive on a strange new planet. *easy*

Sargent, Pamela. ***Earthseed.*** Harper & Row, 1983. Ship is a living machine that has nurtured those born of the genetic banks hurled into space 100 years before. It is necessary for Zoheret and the others to leave the only home they've ever known, but they are afraid. Can Ship devise a sure-fire plan to help these Earthlings before it is too late and ensure the survival of the human race? *difficult*

Science Fiction Booklist

Silverberg, Robert. ***Lord Valentine's Castle.*** Bantam, 1980. Valentine lives on the planet Majipoor, a magical place. In his quest, he joins a troupe of jugglers as they wander from place to place. *difficult*

Slater, Jim. ***The Boy Who Saved Earth.*** Dell, 1979. Earth is in danger of being destroyed. Its only hope for the future rests with a recent alien crash victim who is desperately trying to communicate with his home planet. *average*

Wismer, Donald. ***Starluck.*** Doubleday, 1982. Paul escapes being executed. He joins a secret revolutionary group who are trying to rid their planet of an evil emperor. *easy*

TIME TRAVEL

Curry, Jane Louise. ***Me, Myself and I.*** Margaret K. McElderry, 1987. J. J., who is sixteen, uses his teacher's invention to time travel. *average*

Del Rey, Lester. ***Tunnel through Time.*** Scholastic, 1966. Doc Tom has catapulted through time in a time machine and has entered a primitive era when dinosaurs lived. When Pete realizes his father hasn't returned, he and his friend, Bob, take off to save them. *easy*

Foster, Alan Dean. ***The Last Starfighter.*** Universal City, 1984. The starfighter comes to town to take you back to his world so you can help save it. He knows that you will be a good starfighter, because you are the champion on the electronic game in your hometown. *average*

Gardner, Craig Shaw. ***Back to the Future, Part II.*** Berkley, 1989. In this sequel, Marty McFly somehow never quite makes it to class on time or to dinner for that matter. Then, one day, thanks to Doc Brown and his DeLorean, Marty isn't in school at all. He returns to his past. *average*

L'Engle, Madeline. ***A Wrinkle in Time.*** Farrar, Straus & Giroux, 1962. Meg Murray and her small brother, Charles Wallace, learn how to travel via a tesseract, which is a wrinkle in time. *easy*

Levin, Betty. ***A Griffon's Nest.*** Macmillan, 1975. In this sequel to *The Sword of Culann*, the bronze sword hilt continues to have the power to lead people back through time. Claudia and Evan follow the hilt and find themselves on the Orkney Islands in the seventh and tenth centuries. *difficult*

Mayne, William. ***The Hill Road.*** E. P. Dutton, 1969. Sara finds a magic stone as she and her brother and sister climb the hill for their picnic. Suddenly they are transported to another time in which red-headed Sara has become red-headed Magra. *average*

Ormondroyd, Edward. ***All in Good Time.*** Parnassus Press, 1975. Susan Shaw takes her father in the elevator to help save Mrs. Walker—the elevator that goes up and back in time. This is a sequel to *Time at the Top*. *average*

Wells, H. G. ***The Time Machine.*** *any edition.* It is A. D. 802,701 and the Time Traveller has crossed into a future civilization at war. His time machine is missing and he is unable to return to this planet. *difficult*

© 1993 Patricia S. Morris and Margaret A. Berry

Fantasy Booklist

ANIMALS

Adams, Richard. *Shardik.* Avon, 1976. While hunting, a young hunter finds a large bear and identifies it as an emissary of God. *difficult*

Adams, Richard. *Watership Down.* Macmillan, 1972. This is a tale about a group of rabbits who are leaving their home because of danger. Will they survive in the new society they are establishing? *difficult*

Aiken, Joan. *Arabel's Raven.* Doubleday, 1974. Mortimer is a raven who causes a great deal of change at the Jones' house. *easy*

Arkin, Alan. *The Lemming Condition.* Harper & Row, 1976. This story anthropomorphizes a group of lemmings as they begin their journey toward the sea where they will meet their eventual death. Bubber is fighting his instincts in order to survive. *average*

Bach, Richard. *Jonathan Livingston Seagull.* Avon, 1970. An allegorical short novel of growing up, being the best you can be, and accepting it. *easy*

Baker, Betty. *Dupper.* Greenwillow, 1976. Dupper is off to find the secret to save his community of prairie dogs from the threat of rattlesnakes. *easy*

Bell, Clare. *Ratha and Thistle-Chaser.* Macmillan, 1990. The clan, Named, is headed by the female cat, Ratha. This clan of wildcats is in danger of extinction because of the drought. Scouting parties are sent out to find new sources of food and water. What they also find forces Ratha to search her past, which in turn has a very important impact on the Named. *average*

Brock, Betty. *No Flying in the House.* Harper & Row, 1970. A tiny white dog who appears before Mrs. Vancourt, a rich dowager, announces that she and her companion need a temporary home. *easy*

Butterworth, Oliver. *The Enormous Egg.* Dell, 1978. Nate Twitchell is surprised to find that a dinosaur is his new pet. *easy*

Callen, Larry. *Pinch.* Little, Brown & Co., 1975. Pinch Grimball's pet pig, Homer, helps him hunt birds in Louisiana. *average*

Coatsworth, Elizabeth Jane. *The Cat Who Went to Heaven.* Macmillan, 1967. A small white cat is painted into a picture of a dying Buddha, ensuring that he goes to heaven. *easy*

Donovan, John. *Family: A Novel.* Harper & Row, 1976. Four apes set out to find freedom outside the laboratory only to realize that they are unable to survive in an uncivilized setting. *average*

Grahame, Kenneth. *The Wind in the Willows.* any edition. The lives and times of Ratty, Mole, Badger, Toad, and the other River-Bankers are examined in this classic. *easy*

Hawdon, Robin. *A Rustle in the Grass.* TOR, 1984. A colony of ants awaken from hibernation to find that they are in grave danger. An army of giant red ants are about to attack their quiet, little community. *difficult*

Langton, Jane. *The Fledgling.* Harper & Row, 1980. Georgie's fondest hope, to be able to fly, is fleetingly fulfilled when she is befriended by a Canada goose. *easy*

Le Guin, Ursula. *Catwings Return.* Orchard Books, 1989. This is a sequel to *Catwings*. Wishing to visit their mother, two winged cats

Fantasy Booklist

leave their new country home to return to the city, where they discover a winged kitten in a building about to be demolished. *very easy*

Lively, Penelope. ***The Voyage of QV 66.*** E. P. Dutton, 1979. Set in the future, only animals survive a flood. Six set out to London. *average*

Myers, Walter Dean. ***The Golden Serpent.*** Viking Press, 1980. Even though the mystery of the golden serpent is solved and presented to the king, he still seems unable to comprehend the answer. *average*

O'Brien, Robert C. ***Mrs. Frisby and the Rats of NIMH.*** Atheneum, 1971. Mrs. Frisby rescues a group of genius-level laboratory rats. *easy*

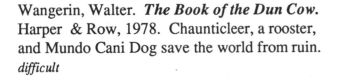

Wangerin, Walter. ***The Book of the Dun Cow.*** Harper & Row, 1978. Chaunticleer, a rooster, and Mundo Cani Dog save the world from ruin. *difficult*

Zindel, Paul. ***Let Me Hear You Whisper.*** Harper & Row, 1974. A cleaning woman realizes that a dolphin, a laboratory subject, is capable of communicating, and she sets out to save its life. *average*

CHEMISTRY

Corbett, Scott. ***The Hairy Horror Trick.*** Scholastic, 1969. The trick is turned on the tricksters. Kerby, Fenton, and Gay wish that they had never attempted to use the chemistry set and with good reason. *easy*

Delaney, Michael. ***Not Your Average Joe.*** E. P. Dutton, 1990. Playing with her brother's old chemistry set, Nicole mixes a formula which makes her uncle's old G. I. Joe doll come alive. *easy*

Hughes, Dean. ***Nutty Knows All.*** Atheneum, 1988. Nutty never meant to design a science project that would create more of a stir than last year's. But, suddenly, he finds that his head glows in the dark and that he is acting differently, thanks to William Bilks. *easy*

COLLECTIONS

Alexander, Lloyd. ***The Foundling and Other Tales of Prydain.*** Holt, Rinehart, & Winston, 1973. This book includes six tales concerning the land of Prydain before Taran's birth. *easy*

Brittain, Bill. ***The Wish Giver.*** Harper & Row, 1983. The Wish Giver is a carney con granting wishes. Only these wishes come true, literally! *easy*

Chrisman, Arthur Bowie. ***Shen of the Sea: Chinese Stories.*** E. P. Dutton, 1926. This is a collection of Chinese legends, often humorous. *average*

Gray, Nicholas. ***A Wind from Nowhere.*** Merrimack, 1979. This book contains humorous fairy tales dealing with demons, dragons, wizards, and royalty. *average*

Gray, Nicholas. ***Mainly in Moonlight.*** Meredith Press, 1967. This book tells ten stories concerning sorcery and the supernatural. *easy*

Kipling, Rudyard. ***Just So Stories.*** Doubleday, 1946. This is a collection of twelve tales including some about a camel, a leopard, and a rhinoceros. *easy*

Kipling, Rudyard. ***The Jungle Book.*** *any edition.* This book tells tales of jungle animals and of a boy who is raised by a pack of wolves. Its sequel is *The Second Jungle Book.* *easy*

Fantasy Booklist

LeGuin, Ursula. ***The Wind's Twelve Quarters: Short Stories.*** Bantam, 1975. This is a collection of seventeen stories of fantasy and science fiction. *diffficult*

McCaffrey, Anne. ***Get off the Unicorn.*** Ballantine, 1971. This is a collection of short stories that deal with unicorns, fantastical creatures, and parapsychic powers. *average*

Sandburg, Carl. ***Rootabaga Stories.*** Harcourt Brace Jovanovich, 1951. This book includes a collection of forty-nine tales. Its sequel is *Rootabaga Pigeons*. *average*

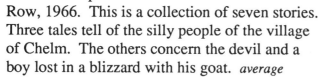

Singer, Isaac Bashevis. ***Zlateh the Goat and Other Stories.*** Harper & Row, 1966. This is a collection of seven stories. Three tales tell of the silly people of the village of Chelm. The others concern the devil and a boy lost in a blizzard with his goat. *average*

Yolen, Jane. ***Dragons and Dreams.*** Harper & Row, 1986. This is a collection of ten original stories that involve time travel, unusual creatures, dreams and magic. *average*

Yolen, Jane. ***Shape Shifters.*** Seabury, 1978. The tales in this book concern humans who are capable of changing their shapes. *average*

COMMUNITY

Cresswell, Helen. ***The Winter of the Birds.*** Macmillan, 1976. Mr. Rudge predicts that evil steel birds will come to town and cause harm. His neighbors unite to defend themselves. *average*

Herbert, Frank. ***Children of Dune.*** Berkley, 1976. Set in the future against the background of an arid land area, coming to life once again, the royal twins Ghanima and Leto use the superior powers inherited from their father to protect their positions in society. This is a continuation of the classic *Dune* story. *difficult*

Jackson, Shirley. ***The Lottery.*** Creative Education, 1983. Written in a creepily matter-of-fact style, this classic horror story focuses on how one society keeps the population down. *easy*

Jones, Diana. ***Drowned Ammet.*** Atheneum, 1978. No one really understands the tradition of the annual festival known as the Holland Sea Festival. During it, two life-size dummies are thrown into the sea. Mitt is drawn into an adventure one festival day when he learns the secrets of Old Ammet and Libby Beer. It will change his life. *average*

Luenn, Nancy. ***Goldclimbers.*** Atheneum, 1991. Aracco always dreams of traveling beyond his village but knows that he must stay and fulfill his expected role as a goldsmith. It is not until the gold reserve is in danger that Aracco is chosen to leave the village. *average*

Pratchett, Terry. ***Diggers.*** Delacorte, 1989. Forced to leave the safety of a department store that had been their home for years, a group of "nomes" finds refuge in a quarry. To the surprise of these four-inch high creatures, life becomes extraordinarily difficult. *average*

Pratchett, Terry. ***Truckers.*** Delacorte, 1989. Reluctant to believe that there's a world outside the department store in which they live, Torrit, Dorcas, and the other "nomes" look to Masklin, a newly arrived outsider, to lead them to safety when their home, the department store, is forced to close. *average*

Fantasy Booklist

Siegel, Maxwell. ***Central Park Underground.*** Dell, 1968. The Central Park Underground is made up of a group of people who live off the land in Manhattan. George Revere joins the group when they nursed him back to health after he was mugged in Central Park, New York City. This is a very unusual approach to surviving in New York. *average*

DEATH and GHOSTS

Alexander, Lloyd. ***The Kestrel.*** E. P. Dutton, 1982. The land of Westmark is plunged into war after the assassin, Skiet, is shot. Mickle and Theo are changed forever because of this. *average*

Arthur, Ruth. ***Miss Ghost.*** Atheneum, 1979. Elpie is lonely in her new boarding school until she meets a ghost who tries to help her develop friendships. *average*

Beagle, Peter. ***A Fine and Private Place.*** Dell, 1960. This story is set in a Bronx cemetery where Michael Morgan and Laura Durand enjoy happiness as spirits. Then one day a body is exhumed and their happiness seems altered forever. *average*

Bellairs, John. ***The Figure in the Shadows.*** Dial, 1975. Chubby Lewis finds a coin in his grandfather's truck and believes it to be filled with magical powers. But, he is not prepared for the strange and eerie events that follow. *easy*

Bellairs, John. ***The Mummy, the Will, and the Crypt.*** Dial, 1983. A will is hidden in the old mansion and Johnny Dixon has figured out its location. He enters the house one night to claim his prize when he suddenly realizes that there is a large form about to attack him. *average*

Boston, L. M. ***The Treasure of Green Knowe.*** Harcourt Brace Jovanovich, 1954. Part of the Green Knowe series, in which Tolly, a young boy, listens to his great-grandmother tell stories about the people who lived in the house a century ago. They come alive for Tolly. *easy*

Butler, Beverly. ***Ghost Cat.*** Scholastic, 1984. Annabel doesn't want to spend the summer with relatives who don't seem to want her there. Suddenly she finds a ghost cat and his mistress who are contacting her for help. The summer becomes more interesting. *easy*

Church, Richard. ***The French Lieutenant: A Ghost Story.*** John Day Company, 1972. Robert doesn't believe the rumors that there is a ghost living in the castle near his home. But, one day he sees the ghost. *average*

Cobalt, Martin. ***Pool of Swallows.*** Thomas Nelson, 1974. Martin watches as the three swallows below the cliff become one and rise to a point where the cows are grazing. They then pull each cow in turn to its death. Are people right? Do ghosts really exist? *average*

Corbett, Scott. ***Captain Butcher's Body.*** Little, Brown & Co., 1976. Captain Butcher, a former pirate, is now a ghost. Every hundred years he makes an appearance and George and Leo can't wait. *easy*

Corbett, Scott. ***The Discontented Ghost.*** E. P. Dutton, 1978. The tale of the Canterville Ghost, an Oscar Wilde story, is retold in first person by Sir Simon de Canterville. *average*

Garfield, Leon. ***Mister Corbett's Ghost.*** Pantheon Books, 1968. Benjamin wishes for the death of his former employer, Mr. Corbett. Mr. Corbett's ghost returns to haunt Benjamin because of this. *average*

Fantasy Booklist

Lawrence, Louise. ***Sing and Scatter Daisies.*** Harper & Row, 1977. Anna is dying but falls in love with a ghost, John Hollis. Her nephew, Nick, is very jealous of their relationship. *average*

Leach, Christopher. ***Rosalinda.*** Warne, 1978. Rosalinda loses both her true love and her life at the age of seventeen. Centuries later, her ghost reaches out to control Anne who now runs Rosalinda's former family home. *average*

Lively, Penelope. ***A Stitch in Time.*** E. P. Dutton, 1976. Maria notices a hundred-year-old photograph in her summer home, and she is convinced that the woman in the photo still resides in the house. *average*

McKillip, Patricia. ***The House on Parchment Street.*** Atheneum, 1978. Carol believes that she sees ghosts in her home but her family doubts her. *average*

Nixon, Joan Lowery. ***Haunted Island.*** Scholastic, 1987. Chris and Amy are staying with their aunt who just bought an old inn and an island. They soon find out that the island is guarded by two ghosts: Joshua Hanover and his mongrel dog, Shadow. *easy*

Passey, Helen K. ***Speak to the Rain.*** Atheneum, 1989. In his grief after the death of his wife, Mr. Miles brings his daughters, Karen and Janna, to a home in the woods. Trapped spirits seeking escape tempt Karen with the promise of a reunion with her mother if she will help them. It is up to Janna to save her family. *average*

Peyton, K. M. ***A Pattern of Roses.*** Crowell-Collier, 1973. A ghost asks Tim to unlock the mystery that surrounds his death. *average*

Raskin, Ellen. ***Figgs and Phantoms.*** E. P. Dutton, 1974. Mona Lisa Newton does not value her family until one day a favorite uncle dies. *average*

Snyder, Zilpha. ***Eyes in the Fishbowl.*** Atheneum, 1974. While shopping, Dion meets a ghost in a local department store. He suspects that she is a spirit because of her unusual behavior. *average*

Snyder, Zilpha. ***The Truth about Stone Hollow.*** Atheneum, 1974. Jason, a newcomer at school, invites Amy to a special place where ghosts from the past visit. *average*

Spearling, Judith. ***The Ghosts Who Went to School.*** Scholastic, 1970. Wilbur and Mortimer are ghosts who are tired of staying home so they set out to haunt a nearby school. *average*

DRAGONS

Fletcher, Susan. ***Dragon's Milk.*** Atheneum, 1989. Kaeldra possesses a special gift. She understands the ways of the dragons. Because of this, she is able to save her sister's life. The just-hatched dragons are known as draclings and are called Embyr, Pyro, and Synge. *average*

McCaffrey, Anne. ***Dragondrums.*** Bantam, 1979. The drums in the distance are signaling

danger for the planet of Pern. Piemur is sent on a secret journey and his mission is to help Pern survive the deadly threadfall. *average*

McCaffrey, Anne. ***Dragonsinger.*** Atheneum, 1977. Part of the Pern series, this story tells of Menolly, who has impressed a fire lizard and who is a student learning to be a harper from the Masterharper on the Planet of Pern. ***Dragonsong*** is another title in the series. *average*

Fantasy Booklist

McCaffrey, Anne. ***The White Dragon.*** Ballantine, 1978. At first, F'lar wants to attack the Threads directly on Red Star, but Red Star's turbulent atmosphere puts all dragonriders in grave danger. Instead, he has begun to spread grubs all over Pern because he has proven that they are capable of both devouring the enemy and restoring the vegetation that the Threads have damaged. *average*

Murphy, Shirley Rousseau. ***The Dragonbards.*** Harper & Row, 1988. Prince Tebriel, a dragonrider and a dragonbard, is exiled from his own land by his father's murderer. He battles his enemies, the men of darkness, who try to destroy bard-visions and magic. *average*

Wrede, Patricia C. ***Searching for Dragons.*** Harcourt Brace Jovanovich, 1991. Concerned that dragons are attempting to destroy part of his kingdom, Mendanbar, the young king of the Enchanted Forest, is sent by Morwen the Witch to King Kazul's castle. There he meets Cimorene, the princess who prefers to call herself Chief Cook and Librarian. This is a sequel to *Dealing with Dragons*. *average*

Yep, Laurence. ***Dragon of the Lost Sea.*** Harper & Row, 1982. A renegade dragon princess, Shimmer, takes a human boy, Thorn, along on her quest to help her kingdom and regain her place among her own. The story is told alternately in first person from both Shimmer's and Thorn's points of view. *average*

Yolen, Jane. ***Dragon's Blood.*** Dell, 1982. It's Jakkin Stewart's wish to escape or earn money to buy his freedom. He must find a hatchling dragon and train him on the sly to fight. This is not an easy task. What if he's unable? Will he never achieve freedom? *average*

Yolen, Jane. ***Heart's Blood.*** Laurel Leaf, 1984. This is a sequel to *Dragon's Blood*. Jakkin is a pitmaster of dragons by day and an undercover agent by night, hoping to discover the whereabouts of Akki, his beloved. *average*

FAMILIES

Aiken, Joan. ***The Shadow Guests.*** Delacorte, 1980. Searching for his mother and older brother, Cosmo learns of a family curse which dooms both. *average*

Cameron, Eleanor. ***Beyond Silence.*** E. P. Dutton, 1980. It seems Andy's nightmares are connected to Scotland and his brother's death. *difficult*

Garfield, Leon. ***Footsteps.*** Yearling, 1980. William Jones knows that the spirit of his dead father will not rest until he makes up for the terrible offense his father committed against Alfred Diamond years before. When William sets out on his journey he has no idea where it will end. *average*

Goudge, Elizabeth. ***Linnets and Valerians.*** Gregg, 1981. The Linnet children are runaways who find a home with Mrs. Valerian. To thank her for her kindness, the children go in search of Mrs. Valerian's son whom she hasn't seen in years. *difficult*

Hamilton, Virginia. ***Sweet Whispers, Brother Rush.*** Philomel Books, 1982. It is through dreams of ghosts that Teresa (Tree) finally understands the tragic events that took place in her mother's family. *difficult*

Hiller, B. B. ***On the Far Side of the Mirror.*** Scholastic, 1986. When Cindy comes to visit she brings the family locket which seems to have magical powers. *easy*

Karl, Jean E. ***Beloved Benjamin Is Waiting.*** E. P. Dutton, 1978. Hounded by a gang of kids

© 1993 Patricia S. Morris and Margaret A. Berry

Fantasy Booklist

after her mother's disappearance leaves her on her own, Lucinda hides in the abandoned caretaker's house in the local cemetery. Here she makes contact with intelligent beings from another galaxy. *average*

Nostlinger, Christine. ***Konrad.*** Avon, 1976. The surprise delivery of a package develops into a mystery when Mrs. Bartolotti realizes that the contents of the package are reconstituted into a son. He is machine made and educated, but suddenly the factory is recalling Konrad. Mrs. Bartolotti refuses to return him and the fun begins. *easy*

Rodgers, Mary. ***Freaky Friday.*** Harper & Row, 1972. Imagine waking up one morning and finding out that you are no longer yourself but rather you are your mother. This is what happened to Annabel Adams. *average*

Sleator, William. ***Singularity.*** E. P. Dutton, 1985. Harry and his twin brother, Barry, house sit a relative's farm. Harry hopes that doing this will bring the two of them back to the closeness they had as children. But the farmhouse is creepy, the playhouse is weird, and strange things start happening. *average*

Springer, Nancy. ***Red Wizard.*** Atheneum, 1990. Ryan, who's just had yet another argument with his dad, finds himself transported into a world with wizards and warlocks. Can he return and will he be able to use the new knowledge about himself? *average*

Wright, Betty. ***Ghosts beneath Our Feet.*** Scholastic, 1984. Katie thinks that staying in the little town of Newquay will help her family become comfortable with one another again. She isn't counting on the danger they are in or the ghost that she will encounter. *easy*

GAMES AND TOYS

Banks, Lynne Reid. ***The Indian in the Cupboard.*** Avon, 1980. Omri really doesn't want the gift of a small plastic figure as his birthday present. But the small figure awakens and takes him on a legendary adventure far beyond his dreams. This is the first in a series. *average*

Clarke, Pauline. ***The Return of the Twelve.*** Coward, McCann & Geoghegan, 1962. Max discovers that wooden soldiers left in an attic 150 years ago by the writer Branwell Bronte are actually alive! He learns their story from them and helps them in their last great adventure. *average*

Cresswell, Helen. ***A Game of Catch.*** Macmillan, 1977. Kate and Hugh are enjoying a game of tag while ice skating when they suddenly encounter the spirits of children who played in the nearby castle in times past. *easy*

Wright, Betty. ***The Doll House Murders.*** Scholastic, 1983. The doll house in the attic holds a secret. Someone from the outer life is trying to send Amy a message, and Amy is frightened. *easy*

HISTORICAL TIMES

Avi. ***Something Upstairs.*** Avon, 1988. When Kenny Huldorf moves to Providence, he doesn't realize that he is also going to move back and forth in time to slave-holding times. Kenny has to believe that ghosts do exist. *easy*

Bellairs, John. ***The Trolley to Yesterday.*** Dial, 1989. Johnny Dixon and Professor Childermas discover a trolley, which transports them back to

Fantasy Booklist

Constantinople in 1453 as the Turks are invading the Byzantine Empire. *average*

Bosse, Malcolm J. ***Cave beyond Time.*** Thomas Y. Crowell, 1980. Set in modern times, Ben, a fifteen-year-old boy, ventures back into primitive times. Here, he experiences the life of a hunter of the tribe of the Waterfall. He learns survival techniques from the nomads, farmers, and hunters he encounters. *average*

Cross, Gilbert. ***A Witch across Time***. Atheneum, 1990. Hannah Kincaid arrived in Stewart's Grove, a 250-year-old Massachusetts estate, ready to put her past behind her. She suddenly finds herself drawn into the Puritan history of her new home and somehow is actually being pulled physically into the past. Will she be able to return? *average*

Dickinson, Peter. ***The Blue Hawk.*** Atlantic-Little, 1976. Tron goes against the wishes of the leaders in ancient Egypt when he saves a hawk that is about to be killed in a religious ritual. *difficult*

DuBois, William. ***The Twenty-One Balloons.*** Viking Press, 1947. Professor Sherman travels in a balloon to see the world. He lands on the volcanic island of Krakatoa in the South Pacific. *average*

King, Stephen. ***The Eyes of the Dragon.*** Viking Press, 1987. Sometimes one must struggle for one's rightful inheritance. Such is the problem of the young prince who lives in the kingdom of Delain. *difficult*

Klaveness, Jan O'Donnell. ***The Griffin Legacy.*** Macmillan, 1983. Lucy Griffin has lived during the American Revolution. She appears before her relative, Amy, begging her to clear the name of her love, Seth, who had been accused of stealing church silver before his death. *average*

Service, Pamela. ***The Reluctant God.*** Atheneum, 1988. While his brother prepares to mount the throne of Egypt, the teenage prince, Ameni, is seated in a secret tomb in a state of suspended animation, to be revived four thousand years later by the fourteen-year-old daughter of an archeologist. *average*

Silverberg, Robert. ***The Gate of the World.*** Holt, Rinehart & Winston, 1967. The Great Plague has caused the deaths of most of the people of Europe during the Middle Ages. *difficult*

Snyder, Zilpha. ***Song of the Gargoyle.*** Delacorte, 1991. Tymmon's father gives up knighthood to become the court jester. Then his father is kidnapped and Tymmon sets out to find him. Instead, he finds himself along the way. *average*

Vinge, Joan. ***Lady Hawke.*** Signet, 1985. Beautiful Isabeau has chosen Etienne Navarre to be her life mate instead of the evil Bishop of Aquila. In turn, the Bishop's curse causes them to wander forever. She becomes a hawk by day and he, a wolf by night. Their only hope is Phillipe, a young thief. *average*

Wallin, Luke. ***The Slavery Ghosts.*** Bradbury Press, 1983. Travelling the tunnels at Tapalyla Hill, Livy and Jake James encounter many ghosts. Some of the spirits need help and pull Livy and Jake into another world. Will their efforts bring hope to the suffering or death to themselves. *average*

Fantasy Booklist

KIDNAPPING

Aiken, Joan. ***Armitage, Armitage, Fly Away Home.*** Doubleday, 1968. Simon arrives in London and is kidnapped, then shipwrecked, as he and his friends, Dido and Justin, set out to discover their true identities. *average*

McKinley, Robin. ***The Blue Sword.*** Greenwillow, 1982. Special powers allow Corlath, the king of the Damarians, to kidnap Harry Crewe. How will she escape? *difficult*

MAGIC

Alexander, Lloyd. ***The Wizard in the Tree.*** E. P. Dutton, 1975. Mallory's encounter with the wizard in the tree begins a chain of events that change the lives of the villagers dominated by a suspicious squire. *average*

Ames, Mildred. ***Conjuring Summer In.*** Harper & Row, 1986. Bernadette is upset over the family's move from Ohio to California. She turns to magic to orchestrate a possible return to Ohio, but, instead, she sets up a situation where she becomes a potential victim of a murderer who has already killed three others. *average*

Avi. ***Bright Shadow.*** Bradbury Press, 1985. Having used four of the five wishes she is granted to make on behalf of the hapless citizens of her country, Morwenna flees the kingdom to decide what to do with the last wish. *easy*

Baker, Margaret J. ***The Sand Bird.*** Thomas Nelson, 1973. When the Minton children find Osborne, the sand-filled glass bird at a rummage sale, they have no idea he is magic and can fulfill their wishes. Oh, but one must be careful of what is wished! *easy*

Bedard, Michael. ***A Darker Magic.*** Atheneum, 1987. A magic show releases an evil force from another world, and suddenly Craig Chandler is in danger of being swept into this dark world. It is up to Miss Potts and Craig's friend, Emily, to save him. *average*

Bellairs, John. ***The House with a Clock in Its Walls.*** Yearling, 1973. Lewis and Uncle Jonathan hear the clock that Isaac Izard has hidden in the walls of Uncle Jonathan's wonderful old house. Each night as it ticks away they both know that it means that each of them is much closer to an untimely death. *average*

Hill, Douglas. ***Master of Fiends.*** Margaret K. McElderry, 1987. Four friends, Jarral, Lady Mandra, Archer, and Scythe, begin a dangerous journey toward the Barrier Peaks to rescue the wizard Cryltaur from the Master of Fiends. *average*

Jones, Diana. ***The Magicians of Caprone.*** Greenwillow, 1980. The Capronas and the Petrocchis had been feuding for so many years that their magical powers began to fail. When an outside source begins to overcome them all, it is up to the younger members of the families to save the day. *average*

Katz, Welwyn. ***The Third Magic.*** Margaret K. McElderry, 1988. Morgan Lefevre is visiting England when she is drawn into another world because of mistaken identity. Morgan is caught between two worlds and she must discover to which she really belongs. *average*

Kooiker, Leonie. ***The Magic Stone.*** Morrow, 1978. Chris finds a magic stone and becomes the focus of interest for an association of witches, one of whom wants him to become her successor. *easy*

LeGuin, Ursula. ***A Wizard of EarthSea.*** Parnassus Press, 1968. Ged is a young boy who is gifted with superior magical powers. As he searches for his true self, he learns from his successes and struggles. Other volumes in this series include *The Tombs of Atuan, The Farthest Shore,* and *Tehanu*. *average*

Fantasy Booklist

Rodgers, Mary. ***A Billion for Boris.*** Harper & Row, 1976. Both Annabel and Boris watch a television set that broadcasts tomorrow's news rather than today's. Boris finds it a perfect way to win at the race track. *average*

White, T. H. ***The Sword in the Stone.*** Dell, 1973. King Arthur learns about magic and history from Merlin, a sorcerer who lives backwards in time. *difficult*

MYSTERY

Babbitt, Natalie. ***Knee-Knock Rise.*** Farrar, Straus & Giroux, 1970. What causes the mysterious wailing sounds that come from the top of Kneeknock Rise? The townspeople call it the Megrimum. *easy*

Hildick, E. W. ***The Ghost Squad Flies Concorde.*** E. P. Dutton, 1985. The Ghost Squad sets out to solve a mystery concerning a thief in England. What they don't count on is the effect that the ghostly supersonic Corrugation Factor will have on them while "hopping" a ride on the Concorde. *easy*

Langton, Jane. ***The Swing in the Summerhouse.*** Harper & Row, 1967. Sequel to *Diamond in the Window*. Young Georgie, sister of Eleanor and Edward, takes her turn on the swing in the summerhouse and disappears. *average*

Wright, Betty. ***The Pike River Phantom.*** Holiday House, 1988. A fast-moving mystery involving a dangerous phantom and two cousins who are desperately trying to stay out of trouble. *easy*

NONFICTION

Day, David. ***A Tolkien Bestiary.*** Ballantine, 1979. This is a guide to all the imaginary monsters, people, places, etc. covered in Tolkien's fantasy worlds. It explains who they are and how they function in his stories. *difficult*

Leach, Maria. ***Standard Dictionary of Folklore, Mythology, and Legend, Vol. 1&2.*** Funk & Wagnalls, 1950. This book comprises information about folklore, mythology, and legends among the various cultures of the world. It is organized alphabetically by name and subject in over 4,000 entries.
difficult

Manguel, Alberto. ***The Dictionary of Imaginary Places.*** Macmillan, 1980. This is a guide to all the wonderful mythical and imaginary places described in literature. *difficult*

Palmer, Robin. ***A Dictionary of Mythical Places.*** Henry Z. Walck, 1975. This is a lexicon or dictionary, that offers description, of mythical, legendary, and famous places. *average*

Post, J. B. ***An Atlas of Fantasy.*** Ballantine, 1979. This book provides the reader with an atlas of maps of imaginary places important in the area of literature. Many are copies of maps from which the author of a book worked while planning and writing about his fanciful places. *average*

Strachey, Barbara. ***Journeys of Frodo: An Atlas of J. R. R. Tolkien's Lord of the Rings.*** Ballantine, 1991. This book maps the journey of Frodo and his friends to Mordor in Tolkien's epic trilogy. It is based directly on information derived from the book's text, and it includes fifty maps.
average

ORPHANS

Cassedy, Sylvia. ***Behind the Attic Wall.*** Avon, 1983. Maggie, an orphan, is a very confused child. Repeatedly thrown out of boarding schools, she does not find peace within herself until her great aunts take her into the ancestral homestead. It is here that she finds her roots. *average*

Fantasy Booklist

Fleischman, Sid. ***Chancy and the Grand Rascal.*** Little, Brown & Co., 1966. Chancy, an orphan, is in search of his biological family and adventure. *easy*

Smith, Stephanie. ***The Boy Who Was Thrown Away.*** Atheneum, 1987. Thrown out by his family at the age of five, Amant is kidnapped by desert raiders, the Dovai, who bring him into the Tribe. The Dovai are attacked and Amant becomes a slave in Mossdon to the Ebsters. Because of his musical ability the Ebsters send him to Kheon, where he finds heartache and his destiny. *average*

OTHER WORLDS

Alexander, Lloyd. ***The Black Cauldron.*** Yearling, 1965. It is necessary that the Black Cauldron, the chief tool of evil used by the corrupt Arawn, be demolished. It is Taran's goal to be the main force in this destruction. *average*

Brooks, Terry. ***Hook.*** Ballantine, 1991. This is a retelling of the Peter Pan story from a grown-up Peter Pan's point of view, with Wendy as a grandmother. *average*

Carroll, Lewis. ***Alice's Adventures in Wonderland*** and ***Through the Looking Glass.*** *any edition.* Alice's curiosity causes her to follow a rabbit into a strange new world where she encounters the Mad Hatter and the Queen of Hearts. Her second adventure takes her through a mirror where she finds a curious backwards world. *average*

Dalton, Annie. ***Out of the Ordinary.*** Harper & Row, 1988. One summer Molly Gurney accepts a job as a governess to escape family problems. What Molly doesn't realize is that her advertisement bridged contact with the otherworld and her new charge, Floris, is now is serious danger. *average*

Delint, Charles. ***The Dreaming Place.*** Atheneum, 1990. Nina's strange dreams suddenly become a reality when she is drawn into an unknown world. Her cousin, Ash, whom she has always despised, is the only one who can save her. *difficult*

Lawrence, Louise. ***Star Lord.*** Harper & Row, 1978. A young man from outer space crashes into the mountains in Wales where Rhys Williams hides him from the British police. *difficult*

LeGuin, Ursula. ***The Beginning Place.*** Bantam, 1981. Irene finds a special place and resents Hugh's knowledge of it. But now they must locate and kill a fearful beast together. *difficult*

Rubinstein, Gillian. ***Space Demons.*** Archway, 1986. Andrew, Ben, and Elaine are engrossed in the new computer game that Andrew's father has brought back from a trip. Suddenly the game becomes all too real and the three are fighting for their lives as they are being drawn into another world. *average*

Sargent, Sarah. ***Jonas McFee, ATP.*** Bradbury Press, 1989. A blue crystal from outer space gives ten year old Jonas McFee more power than he could have ever imagined. *easy*

Snyder, Zilpha. ***Below the Root.*** Atheneum, 1975. Green-Sky, the fantasy world populated by the Kindar, is a land of huge trees with an enormous sky of leafy limbs and a floor of spreading great roots. The Kindar have always been told that monsters lived below the roots. Is it true? *average*

Tolkien, J. R. R. ***The Fellowship of the Ring*** trilogy. Ballantine, 1965. If Sauron and the Ringwraiths are able to discover the ring that Frodo Baggins is carrying, they will have the power to destroy all that is good in the Middle-Earth. So Frodo sets out for Mount Doom where

Fantasy Booklist

the ring can be destroyed and evil can be kept in check. The individual titles in the trilogy are *The Lord of the Rings, The Two Towers,* and *The Return of the King. The Hobbit* can also be read at this time. *difficult*

Wheeler, Thomas. ***Lost Threshold: A Novel.*** Phillips, 1968. James MacGregor is searching for his father when he finds he must enter another world where he becomes a leader and a soldier. *difficult*

PERSONAL CONFLICT

Adler, C. S. ***Eddie's Blue-Winged Dragon.*** G. P. Putnam's Sons, 1988. Eddie is physically challenged and has difficulty in school. Suddenly a purchase of a blue-winged dragon seems to help his problems. But can it really? *easy*

Aiken, Joan. ***Nightbirds on Nantucket.*** Doubleday, 1966. A woman, pretending to be a relative of Dutiful, is planning evil. Although she rescues Dido and Dutiful from the sea, she hopes to hurt King James of England. *average*

Babbitt, Natalie. ***Tuck Everlasting.*** Bantam, 1975. The Tuck family moves quite often and, somehow, doesn't seem to age like everyone else. Do they let anyone else in on the secret? *easy*

Bethancourt, T. Ernesto. ***The Dog Days of Arthur Cane.*** Holiday House, 1976. Arthur is mysteriously turned into his dog and has to solve some pressing problems before the dog pound retires him forever. *average*

Bond, Nancy. ***A String in the Harp.*** Atheneum, 1977. Peter, Becky, and Jen move to Wales when their father accepts a one-year teaching position at the University of Wales. The family is mourning the recent death of their mother and are growing further apart each day. When Peter finds an ancient key that pulls him back through time into the sixth century, it seems as though the children and their father will never be a family again. *average*

Cresswell, Helen. ***The Night Watchmen.*** Macmillan, 1970. Henry learns the secret about the Night Train from two hobos named Josh and Caleb. *average*

Enright, Elizabeth. ***Tatsinda.*** Harcourt Brace Jovanovich, 1963. Carried by an eagle to a land of white-haired, blue-eyed people, Tatsinda is forced to live like an outsider because of her golden hair and brown eyes. *easy*

Knowles, Anne. ***The Halcyon Island.*** Harper & Row, 1981. Ken overcomes his fear of entering the water through the efforts of Giles, who is a ghost. *average*

McKillup, Patricia. ***The Riddle-Master of Hed.*** Atheneum, 1976. Morgan searches for the special meaning of the three stars located on his face. *difficult*

Ryan, Mary C. ***Me Two.*** Little, Brown & Co., 1991. Everyone has a double, but when Wilf accidentally clones himself he finds it more trouble than he expected. *easy*

Severn, David. ***The Girl in the Grove.*** Harper & Row, 1974. After Paul meets Laura, a ghost, he begins to spend a great deal of time with her, much to his girlfriend Jonquil's dismay. *average*

Sudbury, Rodie. ***The Silk and the Skin.*** E. P. Dutton, 1982. Guy Carmichael desperately wants to be part of the group so he allows his brother, who is slightly retarded, to be used to summon ghosts. *average*

Wood, Marcia. ***The Secret Life of Hillary Thorne.*** Macmillan, 1988. The characters from the books Hillary reads become far too real to Hillary. She realizes that her family problems are causing her to escape into other worlds. She

Fantasy Booklist

must find a way to use her imagination to help her in the real world. *average*

ROBOTICS

Bartholomew, Barbara. ***The Great Gradepoint Mystery.*** Macmillan, 1985. Meet ALEC (Access Linkage to Electronic Computer), which is a detective in a computer system. Its purpose is to track the guilty person who is tampering with all of South Side students' grades. *easy*

Bellairs, John. ***The Eyes of the Killer Robot.*** Bantam, 1986. Thirteen-year-old Johnny Dixon is kidnapped for his eyes. The evil Evaristus Stone is known to bring his robots alive through the insertion of human eyes. *easy*

ROYALTY

Aiken, Joan. ***The Cuckoo Tree.*** Doubleday, 1971. It is Dido Twite's intent to push St. Paul's Cathedral into the river. He wants to do this during a royal coronation ceremony. *average*

Colum, Padraic. ***The Boy Apprenticed to an Enchanter.*** Macmillan, 1966. This is a story of magic and enchantment set in a time of kings and magicians and sorcerers. *difficult*

Cooper, Louise. ***The Sleep of Stone.*** Atheneum, 1991. Ghysla's love for Prince Anyr causes her to turn his betrothed into a block of stone. She then assumes Sivorne's identity but lives in fear that her true identity will be discovered. *average*

Lindgren, Astrid. ***Ronia, the Robber's Daughter.*** Viking Press, 1983. Ronia, who lives with her father and his band of robbers in a castle in the woods, causes trouble when she befriends the son of a rival robber chieftain. *easy*

Mayhar, Ardath. ***Makra Choria.*** Atheneum, 1987. The Gift of Makraitis is a power that can be used for good or abused. Two heirs of the ruling family are trained in the power. Theora is the evil sister and Choria sets out to take the power away from her sister. Both sisters have to learn to survive on their own. *average*

McKinley, Robin. ***The Hero and the Crown.*** Greenwillow, 1984. Aerin is the only child of the king of Damar and should be his rightful heir, but she is also the daughter of a witch-woman of the North. *average*

Norton, Andre. ***Wraiths of Time.*** Atheneum, 1976. A strange artifact exposes Tallahassee Mitford to a supply of radiation. It, in turn, takes her to the Nubian kingdom of Meroë. Evil forces cause her to take on the role of Princess Ashake. *difficult*

Peck, Richard. ***Blossom Culp and the Sleep of Death.*** Delacorte, 1986. Blossom Culp finds that she is being haunted by a princess of ancient Egypt who wants to be restored to her rightful tomb. Only Alexander can be counted on to help. *average*

Ruskin, John. ***The King of the Golden River.*** Greenwillow, 1978. The King of the Golden River steps in to stop Gluck's older brothers from distressing him. *easy*

Saint-Exupery, Antoine de. ***The Little Prince.*** Harcourt Brace Jovanovich, 1943. Set in the Sahara, a stranded aviator meets a young boy who relates his many adventures concerning his travels through the universe. *easy*

Thurber, James. ***The 13 Clocks.*** Simon & Schuster, 1950. Prince Zorn wants to marry the princess. To do so, he must complete the task of starting all of the stilled clocks in the area. But, first, he must locate 1,000 jewels. *average*

SUPERNATURAL

Alcock, Vivien. ***The Haunting of Cassie Palmer.*** Dell, 1980. This is a fantasy that

Fantasy Booklist

delves into psychic powers, the supernatural, and the life of a seventh child of a seventh child. A good tale. *easy*

Bellairs, John. ***The Lamp from the Warlock's Tomb.*** Bantam, 1988. A simple lamp, stolen from an underground tomb, possesses power that when unleashed can destroy the world. Anthony and Miss Fells must stop this from happening. *easy*

Boston, L. M. ***The Fossil Snake.*** Atheneum, 1975. Rob puts the rare fossil of a coiled snake he has discovered under the warm radiator in his room. Then a wonderful thing happens. *easy*

Bradbury, Ray. ***The Hallowe'en Tree.*** Alfred A. Knopf, 1972. Will the children come upon a trick or a treat when they encounter the Hallowe'en tree? Does that time of year play any special tricks on the imagination? *average*

Brittain, Bill. ***Devil's Donkey.*** Harper & Row, 1981. Stewmeat and Dan'l realize that they should not have cut branches from Old Magda's tree when Dan'l is turned into a donkey. Is he to remain one forever? *easy*

Brittain, Bill. ***Who Knew There'd Be Ghosts?*** Harper & Row, 1985. Three spunky youngsters join forces with two lively ghosts to save a historic mansion from being destroyed by a crooked antique dealer. *easy*

Chase, Mary. ***The Wicked Pigeon Ladies in the Garden.*** Alfred A. Knopf, 1968. Maureen Swanson, who is called "Old Stinky" by her enemies and doesn't have any friends, invades an abandoned house that everyone calls haunted. *easy*

Conford, Ellen. ***Genie with the Light Blue Hair.*** Bantam, 1989. Jeannie Warren receives a wonderful birthday present from her aunt: a genie who grants wishes. The only trouble is that the genie is a little out of practice. *average*

Coontz, Otto. ***Isle of the Shapeshifters.*** Bantam, 1985. Twelve-year-old Theo arrives on the island for summer vacation. Suddenly she begins to feel that she is being pulled to her death by very strange and mysterious forces. *average*

Downer, Ann. ***The Spellkey.*** Atheneum, 1987. Badger has been sent to take Caitlin, who has been accused of witchcraft, to a convent in Ninthstile. On the way they encounter incredible people and adventures and even fall in love. *average*

Hambly, Barbara. ***Those Who Haunt the Night.*** Ballantine, 1988. Professor James Asher answers the call for help from the vampires in the area. Someone is out to rid London of all of them. But, if Asher succeeds, will the vampires repay him through his own death because now he will have too much knowledge of them? *difficult*

Harris, Rosemary. ***The Seal-Singing.*** Macmillan, 1971. Miranda's unusually close resemblance to a former relative indicates that she might have powers beyond the norm. *difficult*

Hauff, Wilhelm. ***Dwarf Long-nose.*** Random House, 1960. A wonderful tale about a spell cast upon a twelve-year-old boy that transforms him into a misshapen, long-nosed dwarf. *easy*

Hunter, Mollie. ***A Stranger Came Ashore.*** Harper & Row, 1975. Only Robbie fears for his sister's life. He suspects that the man his sister intends to marry may, in fact, be the Great Selkie, known for taking young girls to the bottom of the sea. *difficult*

Fantasy Booklist

Katz, Welwyn. *False Face.* Margaret K. McElderry, 1987. Digging up an Indian mask disturbs the spirits. The supernatural power invested in an Iroquois mask impresses two teenagers who have found the mask in London, Ontario, where they live. *average*

Kay, Mara. *A House Full of Echoes.* Crown Publishers, 1980. When Astrovo, a once-splendid country estate, is turned into Mme. Malvina's boarding school, the occult spirits arrive. *average*

King, Stephen. *The Dead Zone.* Signet, 1979. Johnny falls on the ice and gets a lump on his head. And now grown-up John Smith has the faculty of knowing some things before they happen. *difficult*

Lawrence, Louise. *The Earth Witch.* Harper & Row, 1981. Owen falls in love as spring draws near, but his love leaves him. *difficult*

Mahy, Margaret. *The Changeover.* Scholastic, 1974. Laura knows that Sorenson Carlisle was a witch. What does Sorry say to that? *average*

Naylor, Phyllis. *The Witch Herself.* Dell, 1978. When Lynn's mother, Mrs. Morley, decides to move her writing studio to Mrs. Tuggle's home, the girls fear for Mrs. Morley's safety. They set out to thwart Mrs. Tuggle's witchlike powers before it's too late. *average*

Riddell, Ruth. *Shadow Witch.* Atheneum, 1989. Drew wonders about his survival as he repeatedly meets the shadow witch in his dreams. Are his hallucinations the result of earlier use of LSD? Or is there another reason locked in the family memory? *average*

Sleator, William. *The Boy Who Reversed Himself.* E. P. Dutton, 1986. Omar, Laura's next door neighbor, is weird. Laura starts finding notes in her locker with backwards writing on them. Is it Omar? *average*

Sobol, Donald J. *The Amazing Power of Ashur Fine.* Macmillan, 1986. Ashur Fine's aunt, a private investigator, is mugged while on the way to serve papers on a witness. He sets out to find the person who hurt his aunt. Ashur feels that he has been given special supernatural powers to achieve his goal. *easy*

Wrightson, Patricia. *Balyet.* Margaret K. McElderry, 1989. Little did Jo know that when she hid in the back of her neighbor's car she would encounter the thousand-year-old spirit of Balyet, a young girl who had been banished by her tribe. Suddenly Jo finds herself in danger. *easy*

TIME TRAVEL

Chetwin, Grace. *Collidescope.* Bradbury Press, 1990. When his spaceship crashes to Earth, a highly advanced alien interferes with the lives of two teenagers living on the island of Manhattan during different centuries. *average*

Juster, Norton. *The Phantom Tollbooth.* Random House, 1961. Milo is given a tollbooth as a gift. He finds that this allows him entry into an adventurous land, very different from any he has ever experienced before. *average*

Silverberg, Robert. *Letters from Atlantis.* Atheneum, 1990. Roy travels through time to visit the city of Atlantis. He is amazed at what he finds. *average*

Swift, Jonathan. *Gulliver's Travels into Several Remote Nations of the World.* E. P. Dutton, 1957. Gulliver's ship is destroyed and he lands on the island of Lilliput, a nation of very small people. He then travels to the area of the giants, Brobdingnags. *difficult*

Fantasy Booklist

TREASURE

Fleischman, Sid. ***The Ghost in the Noonday Sun.*** Little, Brown & Co., 1965. In order to locate buried treasure, some pirates abduct Oliver Finch in the hopes that he can obtain treasure clues from the spirit of Gentleman Jim. *easy*

Garfield, Leon. ***The Ghost Downstairs.*** Pantheon Books, 1972. Dennis Fast relinquishes seven years of his life and in return obtains approximately two million dollars. He soon finds out that the seven years he has given up are the first seven years of his life. The ghost of his own childhood haunts him because of this. *average*

Harris, Christie. ***Secret in the Stlalakum Wild.*** Atheneum, 1972. Spirits visit Morann, a Northwest Coast Salish Indian, and she sets out to locate buried treasure. *easy*

Hilton, James. ***Lost Horizon.*** Morrow, 1936. A plane crashes and four survive. They travel to place called Shangri-La where everyone remains eternally young. All four desire to go home, however. *difficult*

Langton, Jane. ***The Diamond in the Window.*** Harper & Row, 1962. Fantastic things happen to Eleanor and Edward as they search for fabulous treasure, for the Indian prince with rubies in his pockets, and for the lost children who disappeared so long ago. *easy*

Levitin, Sonia. ***Jason and the Money Tree.*** Harcourt Brace Jovanovich, 1974. When eleven-year-old Jason plants a money tree, he finds himself in conflict with both the law and nature. *easy*

Stahl, Ben. ***Blackbeard's Ghost.*** Houghton Mifflin, 1965. Blackbeard appears when he realizes that his old tavern is about to be torn down. *average*

Thurber, James. ***The Wonderful O.*** Simon & Schuster, 1957. It seems as though Wicked Black and his fellow pirates have set out to devastate everything spelled with a letter O. *average*

UNICORNS

Beagle, Peter. ***The Last Unicorn.*** Ballantine, 1968. Schmendreck is only a mediocre magician, but he is a very loyal friend to the Last Unicorn. Together, with Molly Grue, they set out on a quest to locate other unicorns. *average*

Cohen, Barbara. ***Unicorns in the Rain.*** Atheneum, 1982. A parable with a Noah twist this adventure involves unicorns, love, and danger which brings Nikki to question her own world. *average*

Lee, Tanith. ***Black Unicorn.*** Atheneum, 1991. Tanaquil, the daughter of a sorceress, is upset because she does not possess a scrap of magic. She can, however, mend anything. That is just what she does with a unicorn skeleton. The resulting black animal seeks Tanaquil, but she is not sure why. *average*

Science Fiction and Fantasy -- Teacher's Notes

CONCEPTS

- Recognition of the characteristics that define science fiction and fantasy.
- Recognition of the purposes of science fiction and fantasy.

OBJECTIVES

The student will:
1. Identify the story elements of science fiction and fantasy including: characters, plot, time setting, place setting.
2. Identify the story line including: conflict, climax, denouement or ending.
3. Identify the literary elements common to most literary types including: foreshadowing, theme, tone, mood, point of view, flashbacks.
4. Identify the particular character of science fiction as fiction that takes the technology or scientific theory of today and projects it into the future in a plausible way.
5. Identify the particular essence of fantasy to be fiction that breaks the laws of nature as we know them, including, for example, dragons, fairies, and/or gnomes.
6. Identify settings of science fiction as anywhere on earth or in space.
7. Identify that settings of fantasy often take place in "other worlds" that are reached through a symbolic bridge.
8. Identify themes of science fiction and fantasy as social problems of today that are creatively addressed.
9. Use library skills to locate and retrieve books and information.
10. Use critical thinking skills and expressive and effective writing.

TEACHER PREPARATION

- There are **two** separate booklists, one each for fantasy and science fiction. Similarly, **two** sets of activities exist, one for fantasy and one for science fiction. You will need to review the student booklists from which students may choose their reading material. Students are free to choose books on their own and can still be assigned the activities, because they are generic, not geared to specific titles.
- Be sure to use union library catalogs and interlibrary loan to access some of the titles.
- You will also need to review the "Keeping Track of Your Choices" sheet on page 2, which includes directions and can be given to the student before he/she chooses a book. Depending on your needs, you may want to modify this sheet. The student will record the book information in duplicate and give you a copy.
- You can then look through the range of activities for science fiction and fantasy and jot down on your copy which activities the student needs. You will then be able to duplicate the activities and give them to the student.
- As a beginning group activity, do SF-1 or FF-1 on a short story that has already been read by the class. These can be employed repeatedly because of their basic nature.
- *Easy, Average,* and *Difficult,* in the table of contents, indicate the relative level of difficulty of the activity sheets. The degree of difficulty was determined by the complexity of the skill or the number of steps to be accomplished.

SF - 1

Name _____ Section _____ Date _____

What Is a Science Fiction Story?

1. After filling in the author and title below, describe the main character and his/her/its daily activities:

2. What is the setting?
   Time:

   Place:

3. What are the major story problems (conflicts)?

4. What are the minor story problems (conflicts)?

5. How are they resolved?

6. What makes this book science fiction?

Title: _____

Author: _____

© 1993 Patricia S. Morris and Margaret A. Berry

					SF - 2

Name _____ Section _____ Date _____

Write Yourself into the Story

Select a science fiction book whose theme is important to your own life. Write a brief chapter putting yourself into the story. Show how you might have helped the character(s) had you been there. Plan your chapter below.

Character(s):

Theme:

How do you fit into the story?

Turning points in the story where you might have made a difference (and what you would have done):

Turning Point	My Action

How would your actions change the outcome of the story?

Title: _____

Author: _____

	SF - 3

Name _____ Section _____ Date _____

Picture This

Select a character from your book. List reasons why you would or would not want this person as a friend or a next-door neighbor. Then go through magazines and cut out words that you feel accurately describe him or her. On a large sheet of paper, draw a picture of how he/she might have looked according to how he/she was described in the story. Write or paste words to create a "mat" for your "picture." Then frame.

Character:

I would want this person as a friend.   Yes   No
I would want this person as a next-door neighbor.   Yes   No

Reasons:
1.

2.

Using this as a model, plan your picture for an 8 ½ x 11 sheet of paper:

picture

mat

Title: _____

Author: _____

© 1993 Patricia S. Morris and Margaret A. Berry

	SF - 4

Name _____ Section _____ Date _____

Writing Dialogue

Either alone or with someone else who has also read the book, write out a scene from any part of your book (with only two characters speaking). Write the dialogue below and describe the actions:

Characters:	Setting:
Action	
Character #1:	
Character #2:	
Dialogue	
Character #1:	
Character #2:	
Character #1:	
Character #2:	
Character #1:	
Character #2:	
Character #1:	
Character #2:	
Character #1:	
Character #2:	
Character #1:	

Title: _____

Author: _____

© 1993 Patricia S. Morris and Margaret A. Berry

SF - 5

Name _____ Section _____ Date _____

Graphing Suspense

Use the science fiction book that you have just finished. By chapter, chart the level of suspense on a line graph including the eventual climax, or high point. In one word on the vertical lines provided below the graph, describe the basic action in each chapter.

High

Medium

Low

Action

Title: _____

Author: _____

© 1993 Patricia S. Morris and Margaret A. Berry

SF - 6

Name _____ Section _____ Date _____

More Time for a Minor Character

Add another scene to the science fiction book you are reading. The scene will be about one of the minor characters and could be a better resolution to the minor character's dilemma. Use the space below to outline your scene briefly.

Minor character:

Other characters:

Story conflict:

New Scene Outline:

New Scene Ending:

Title: _____

Author: _____

© 1993 Patricia S. Morris and Margaret A. Berry

SF - 7

Name_____ Section _____ Date _____

Develop a Survey, Part I

After reading a science fiction book, identify the author's message or theme. Then develop a survey of questions on that topic to give to your classmates. Use questions that can be answered by yes or no. Survey your classmates and tally the answers on SF-8.

THEME:
Questions for the survey:
1.
2.
3.
4.
5.
6.
7.
8.

Title: _____

Author: _____

© 1993 Patricia S. Morris and Margaret A. Berry

SF - 8

Name _____ Section _____ Date _____

Develop a Survey, Part II

From the answers to the survey questions you developed on Activity SF-7, report your findings on a bar graph. Develop a summary paragraph.

1. yes / no
2. yes / no
3. yes / no
4. yes / no
5. yes / no
6. yes / no
7. yes / no

0   5   10   15   20   25   30   35   40   45   50

Write your summary paragraph on the back.

Title: _____

Author: _____

© 1993 Patricia S. Morris and Margaret A. Berry

SF - 9

Name _____ Section _____ Date _____

Impact of Setting

Describe the setting of the book. Now move it to a different setting. You can move around in time as well as location. Describe how this might have changed the course of the entire story.

Characters and conflict: _____

_____

_____

Setting: _____

Major events: _____

_____

_____

New setting:

How would this have changed:
The story?

The ending?

The meaning?

Title: _____

Author: _____

© 1993 Patricia S. Morris and Margaret A. Berry

	S F - 10

Name _____ Section _____ Date _____

Glossary

Using a science fiction book that does not contain a glossary, develop a glossary of at least eight to ten important terms for your book. If you consider your glossary a necessary addition to the book you have just read, leave it with the library media specialist to add to the book.

GLOSSARY:

Term	page #	definition	Did the author invent this word?

Title: _____

Author: _____

S F - 11

Name _____ Section _____ Date _____

Topical Questions and Research

Identify the topic of your science fiction book. After reading it, structure questions that will help you gather information on the current status of that topic. Develop a list of the books that you would use from the reference collection to answer these questions. Examples of topics include, but are not limited to: the aftermath of a nuclear war, space stations, cybernectics, robotics, antimatter propulsion, genetics, artificial intelligence, and ESP..

TOPIC:

Questions:

1.

2.

3.

4.

List of reference books:	Reasons for using

Title: _____

Author: _____

© 1993 Patricia S. Morris and Margaret A. Berry

S F - 15

Name _____ Section _____ Date _____

Technology

Pick an invention in your book and find out whether it is actually possible, theoretically or practically.

Invention: _____

Use: _____
_____
_____
_____

Drawing:

Does it exist in any form today? _____
_____
_____

Has it ever been produced? _____
_____

Could it be produced? _____
_____
_____

Sources consulted: _____

Title: _____

Author: _____

© 1993 Patricia S. Morris and Margaret A. Berry

S F - 16

Name _____ Section _____ Date _____

The Science in Science Fiction

Find a scientific principle or major scientific idea that is important to the technology/setting/plot of your book. Explain in what ways the principle is important.

Principle:

Example of how it is used in book:

How it is important:

Explanation:

Sources:

Title: _____

Author: _____

© 1993 Patricia S. Morris and Margaret A. Berry

	S F - 17

Name _____ Section _____ Date _____

What Does Society Think?

Based on the science fiction book you have read, select a social issue or social conflict. After filling in the items listed below, use your answers to compare and contrast society's attitude in response to the social issue or conflict in a paragraph on the back of this sheet.

Social issue or conflict (A summary including why, who, how):

Society's response in the future: _____
_____
_____
_____
_____
_____
_____

Society's response now: _____
_____
_____
_____
_____
_____
_____
_____

Compare and contrast the two responses in a short, well-written paragraph on the back of this paper.

Title: _____

Author: _____

© 1993 Patricia S. Morris and Margaret A. Berry

S F - 18

Name _____ Section _____ Date _____

Do Aliens Have Emotions?

Identify an alien being from the science fiction book you have read. Describe him/her/it in terms of emotional qualities. Would you want this being as a teacher? Explain in a well-reasoned paragraph.

Identify: _____

Describe:

    Physical:

    Emotional:

Would you want this being as a teacher? Why or why not?

Title: _____

Author: _____

© 1993 Patricia S. Morris and Margaret A. Berry

			S F - 19

Name _____ Section _____ Date _____

A Ticket To Ride

Based on the science fiction book you finished, you will respond to the following. You will board a science fiction transport and you must be able to blend in with the society in your book. Create a costume and/or mask that will allow you to do this.

Society from book: _____

Describe it in detail:

Mask: Draw and describe the colors and textures that do not show. If you have included any moving parts, describe how they will work.

Title: _____

Author: _____

S F - 20

Name_____ Section _____ Date _____

What Are My Rights?

If your science fiction story takes place in a specialized colony or has an organization or structure that is different from the world you know, create a document listing ten rights that the individuals in this society have. If this society has different classes of people with different rights, list them also. Then list your rights as an individual. Finally, in a well-reasoned paragraph on the back of this paper, compare and contrast these rights, discussing which are better or worse.

Individual Rights in the Book's Society	Your Rights Now
1.	
2.	
3.	
4.	
5.	
6.	
7.	
8.	
9.	
10.	

Title: _____

Author: _____

© 1993 Patricia S. Morris and Margaret A. Berry

Name _____ Section _____ Date _____

S F - 21

Real Estate

You are a real estate agent in the time and place setting of your science fiction story. You have three living areas to sell from the book's various locations. Create newspaper real estate listings for each along with a line drawing for each. Include the address in the ad.

Time:

Place:

Drawing	Written Ad

Title: _____

Author: _____

© 1993 Patricia S. Morris and Margaret A. Berry

49

SF - 22

Name _____ **Section** _____ **Date** _____

Transportation

List the methods of transportation for individuals, small groups, larger groups, and freight from your science fiction book.

What are the rules governing transportation?

	Methods	Rules
Individuals		
Small Groups		
Larger Groups		
Freight		

What changes can you foresee in the near future that will be technologically and economically feasible? _____

_____
_____
_____
_____
_____
_____

Title: _____

Author: _____

© 1993 Patricia S. Morris and Margaret A. Berry

Name _____ Section _____ Date _____

Whether Weather

Weather or climate plays a factor in many science fiction stories. List types of climate from your science fiction story in the Effect column.

What is happening in our environment today that might cause this change? List these in the Cause column.

Cause	Effect

On the back of this paper in a short, well-constructed paragraph of cause and effect, explain your findings.

Title: _____

Author: _____

S F - 23

© 1993 Patricia S. Morris and Margaret A. Berry

| S F - 24 |

Name _____ Section _____ Date _____

Interpreting the Story

Based on your book, brainstorm four discussion questions about the meaning of the story for a class discussion. Interpretation questions require questioning the words that the author uses, the way certain things are characterized, or what the connections are between various parts of the story. You must also question what in the story caused you to react or respond a certain way. What was it that the author did? Interpretation questions have no right or wrong answer. As a matter of fact, there are probably several good answers for each one. You can also question what seems important or what you don't understand. Your questions can begin with the word "why".

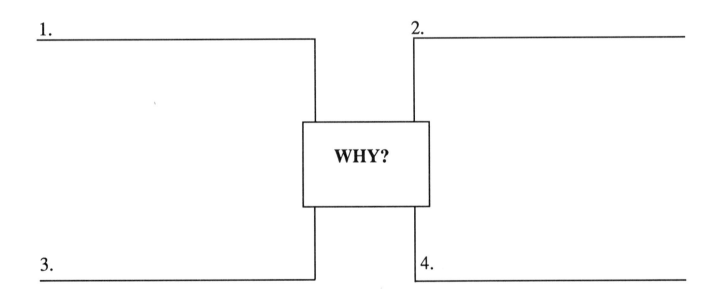

Think about the answers and write them on another piece of paper. Attach to this activity and hand in.

Title: _____

Author: _____

© 1993 Patricia S. Morris and Margaret A. Berry

S F - 25

Name _____ **Section** _____ **Date** _____

Author's Information

Search out information on the author of the science fiction book you are reading. Use *Junior Authors, Something About the Author,* etc. Analyze the background information. List other books the author has written, separating them into different genres, if possible.

Summary, or synopsis, of story: _____
_____

Author: _____
Author's life story, both personal and professional (be sure to include pseudonyms or pen names, other books written, and awards received):
_____
_____
_____
_____
_____
_____

Examine the life story and select two reasons why the author became successful in this career:

1.

2.

Sources:

Title: _____

Author: _____

© 1993 Patricia S. Morris and Margaret A. Berry

S F - 26

Name _____ Section _____ Date _____

Dear Auntie,

You are one of the characters in the science fiction story. Your favorite aunt on Earth writes you a letter inviting you to live with her. Write a letter back to her, stating your reasons for wishing to leave and come live with her, or why you wish to stay and why you must turn her offer down.

Your science fiction story setting:

_____
_____
_____

Dear Aunt,

Sincerely,

Title: _____

Author: _____

© 1993 Patricia S. Morris and Margaret A. Berry

S F - 27

Name _____ Section _____ Date _____

Aliens in the Kitchen

Take two or more of the aliens in your science fiction book and bring them back into your own society. List all of the difficulties they might have based on your knowledge of their characters. Think in terms of housing, food, clothing, social interaction, language, etc.

Aliens	Difficulties	Reasons

Title: _____

Author: _____

© 1993 Patricia S. Morris and Margaret A. Berry

SF - 28

Name _____ Section _____ Date _____

Progress?

Note changes in technology from our time to that of your science fiction novel and the impact those changes have had on the society of your novel. Then, on the back of this paper, compare and contrast your findings.

Technological changes	Impact?
Communication	
Money or Monetary transactions	
Entertainment	
Computers/Artificial Intelligence	
Medicine/Genetics	
Education	
Safety	
Shelter	
Clothing	

Title: _____

Author: _____

	SF - 29

Name _____ Section _____ Date _____

A "Classy" Society

Consider the classes of people in our society (for instance, the working poor, the middle class, the rich). To which classes of society do the individuals in your science fiction book belong? Name and describe from both societies. Is there movement between the classes? How does it occur? Include description of movement.

Now (in United States/Canada):	In the book:

Title: _____

Author: _____

FF - 1

Name_____ Section_____ Date_____

What Is That Fantasy Book About?

1. After filling in the author and title below, name and describe the characters in this book: _____
_____

2. What are the daily activities of the main characters?

3. What is the time setting? _____

4. What is the place setting? _____

5. What are the main conflicts, or story problems?

6. How is the main conflict resolved?

7. What makes this particular story a fantasy?

Title: _____

Author: _____

© 1993 Patricia S. Morris and Margaret A. Belly

FF - 2

Name _____ Section _____ Date _____

Sequence Into a Cartoon

Identify the general sequence of the fantasy book that you just read and develop it into a single-panel cartoon.

Characters:

With words or brief phrases, fill in the boxes below to identify the sequence.

Brainstorm ideas for a cartoon:

Draw your cartoon here:

Title: _____

Author: _____

© 1993 Patricia S. Morris and Margaret A. Berry

FF - 3

Name _____ Section _____ Date _____

Writing a Newspaper Article

Based on your fantasy book, write a lead paragraph to a newspaper article, describing an event from the story. Be sure to include the information that answers: who, what, where, when, how, and sometimes, why.

Who: _____
_____

What: _____
_____

Where: _____
_____

When: _____
_____

How: _____
_____

Why: _____
_____

Lead paragraph:

Title: _____

Author: _____

FF - 4

Name _____ Section _____ Date _____

Bulletin Board Fantasy

Create a bulletin board based on your fantasy book. Develop it in miniature by doing a draft on this page. Submit it for approval.

Characters:

Setting
   Time: _____
   Place: _____

Plot: _____
_____
_____

Brainstorm bulletin board ideas:

Develop your bulletin board here by sketching three or four ideas. Then star the one you will do.

Title: _____

Author: _____

© 1993 Patricia S. Morris and Margaret A. Berry

FF - 5

Name _____ Section _____ Date _____

Periodical Search

Determine the author's theme. Translate the theme into a topic that is relevant to a social issue today. Look in the multiple periodical indexes in the library including: *Magazine Article Summaries, Readers' Guide, Current Biography, WilsonDisc, American Heritage,* and *National Geographic.* Develop a bibliography of possible article citations for further research based on the topic or theme. *Example: Overcoming barriers or handicaps might be translated into Rights of the Handicapped, Wheelchair barriers.*

Characters: _____

Setting: _____

Plot: _____

Theme: _____

Social issue: _____

Topic to look up: _____

Readers' Guide: _____

Magazine Article Summaries: _____

WilsonDisc: _____

Dialog: _____

American Heritage: _____

Current Biography: _____

National Geographic: _____

Title: _____

Author: _____

© 1993 Patricia S. Morris and Margaret A. Berry

FF - 6

Name _____ Section _____ Date _____

Filmstrip

In the large frames 1-8, create a filmstrip based on the fantasy you are reading. In the small frames 1-8, write a caption for each.

Characters: _____
Setting:
   Time: _____
   Place: _____

Plot: _____

Theme: _____

Filmstrip:

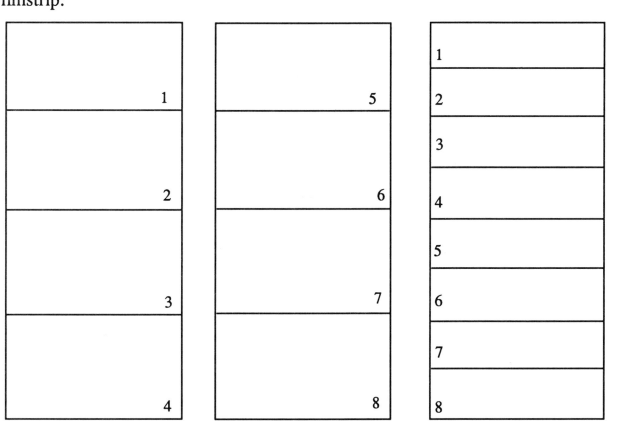

Title: _____

Author: _____

FF - 7

Name _____ Section _____ Date _____

Changing the Ending

After reading your fantasy book, develop or describe an invention that might have changed the ending of the story.

Characters: _____

Time/Place: _____

Plot: _____

Invention:
   Describe, draw, and explain:
   _____
   _____
   _____
   _____
   _____
   _____
   _____
   _____

How could it have changed the ending?

Title: _____

Author: _____

© 1993 Patricia S. Morris and Margaret A. Berry

Name _____ Section _____ Date _____

FF - 8

Fantasy Mobile

Make a mobile based on all the fanciful or magical aspects of the work you have just read. Plan your mobile below.

Fanciful aspects:
_____
_____
_____
_____
_____
_____

Title: _____

Author: _____

© 1993 Patricia S. Morris and Margaret A. Berry

FF - 9

Name_____ Section _____ Date _____

Advertising

Videotape advertisements of the class's favorite book choices in the fantasy area. Use the space below to storyboard your advertisement for the fantasy that you have read.

Pictures/Camera Shots	Words/Sound

© 1993 Patricia S. Morris and Margaret A. Berry

Title: _____

Author: _____

Name _____ Section _____ Date _____

Good vs. Evil

From the fantasy story which you have finished, place three characters on the continuum of good ←――→ evil. Explain why in the boxes below, making sure that you use the names of the characters.

Totally good ←――――――――――――――――――→ Totally evil

Explanation:

Character #1	Character #2	Character #3

Title: _____

Author: _____

FF - 10

FF - 11

Name _____ Section _____ Date _____

Real vs. Unreal

During your reading of the fantasy story, you came across words and phrases which were not familiar. In the circle below, place the words or phrases which represent the real world. In the box surrounding the circle, place the words or phrases which, to you, represent the unreal world. Use a dictionary to make sure. Define the unreal world words and phrases on the back of this paper.

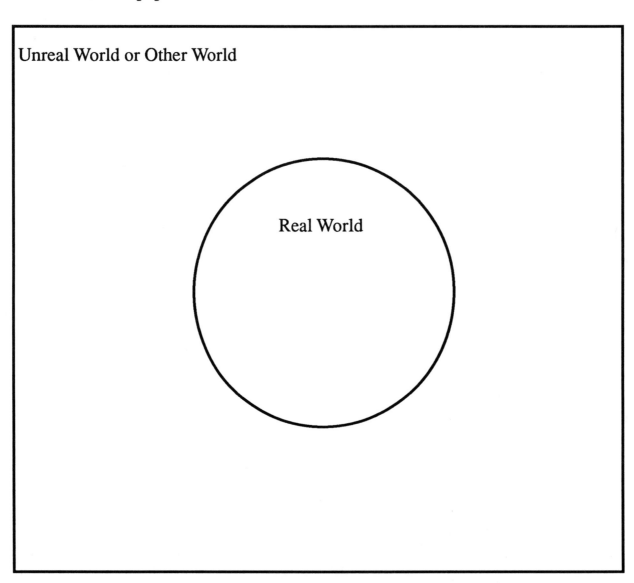

Title: _____

Author: _____

© 1993 Patricia S. Morris and Margaret A. Berry

Name _____ Section _____ Date _____

Bridging the Two Worlds

If your fantasy fiction alternates between the everyday real world and a secondary, other world, there will be some kind of bridge or symbol which permits entry into the secondary world and sometimes a different one which allows return into the real world. In the top box, describe the everyday world of the book, including setting and characters. In the bottom box, describe the secondary or other world in the same way. Between the two, describe the symbol that bridges both worlds, triggering entry into the other world and exit back, and indicate how many times it is used.

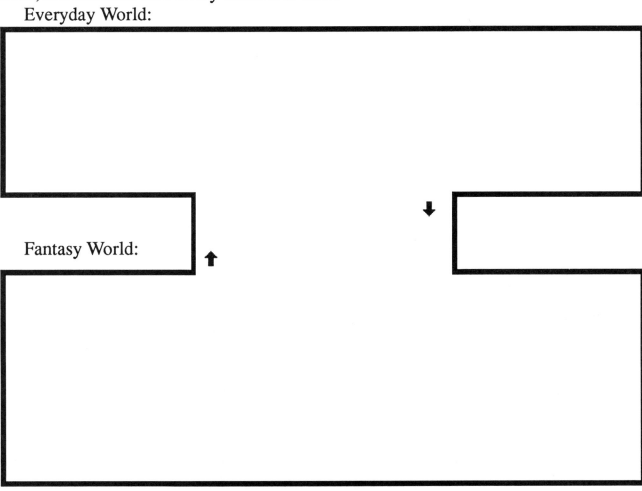

Occasionally, a symbol which forbids the entrance or exit into the other worlds is used. On the back of this paper, draw and explain this symbol.

Title: _____

Author: _____

FF - 13

Name _____ Section _____ Date _____

Categories of Themes

After finishing fantasy fiction, survey your classmates and place their book choices in the correct category. Add more columns as necessary. This can be used as a bulletin board on which you can identify outstanding books recommended by your classmates.

Good vs. evil	*Power corrupts*	*Greed is bad*

Quest	*Love overcomes*	*Discovering True Values*

Fighting for One's Place	*Healing*	*Other*

Identify with a star those books which are strongly recommended.

Title: _____

Author: _____

© 1993 Patricia S. Morris and Margaret A. Berry

		FF - 14

Name _____ Section _____ Date _____

Fantasy Symbols

A symbol can be any concrete item including an emblem, a badge, a letter, a token, a device, a character, a mark, an animal, or anything that points to the meaning of the symbol. Interview your classmates who have read fantasy and fill in the chart below. Remember the same symbol can be used in many different ways and mean something different to each fantasy. *Example: A ring is used as a symbol in both* The Hobbit *and* The Hundredth Dove, *but with different meanings.*

Identify: The symbol	The story	The meaning	The importance

In a well written paragraph on the back of this paper, identify surprising aspects of a symbol in the story.

Title: _____

Author: _____

FF - 15

Name_____ Section _____ Date _____

Changing a Symbol

Based on the symbol or device in your fantasy story, create another which would have worked as well.

Book's symbol:

Symbol's meaning:

Symbol's effect:

New symbol:

New symbol's meaning:

New symbol's effect:

Title: _____

Author: _____

© 1993 Patricia S. Morris and Margaret A. Berry

FF - 16

Name _____ Section _____ Date _____

Outlining a New Chapter

Based on the ending of the story, plan another chapter to include in your fantasy. The new chapter might develop a minor character or a minor event and can be inserted anywhere within the story. Be sure the chapter is true to the same theme, plot, and characterizations.

Characters:

Plot:

Theme:

NEW CHAPTER

Characters' development
   1.

   2.

   3.

Plot outline for new chapter:

On the back of this paper write a paragraph about any new characters you added.

Title: _____

Author: _____

© 1993 Patricia S. Morris and Margaret A. Berry

FF - 17

Name _____ Section _____ Date _____

Outlining a Sequel

Since many fantasies are parts of series, outline a possible sequel to your fantasy book, one that the author, to the best of your knowledge, has not already written. Before you begin, fill out the information requested below.

Book's main characters: _____

Theme: _____

Setting (time/place): _____

New main characters added (names and descriptions): _____
_____
_____
_____

Theme: _____

Setting (time/place): _____
_____

Plot outline: _____
_____
_____
_____
_____
_____
_____
_____

Title: _____

Author: _____

© 1993 Patricia S. Morris and Margaret A. Berry

FF - 18

Name _____ Section _____ Date _____

New Scene

After finishing your fantasy, perhaps there might be something that you would like to add to the story. Create a scene between a fantastical creature and the major character that the author has not written in the story.

Fantasy creature: _____

Major character and conflict: _____
_____
_____
_____

Where will you insert the new scene you are creating? (What comes just before and after it?) _____
_____
_____

Describe who is in the scene, what happens, where it takes place, how it comes out.
_____
_____
_____
_____
_____
_____
_____
_____
_____
_____
_____
_____
_____
_____

Title: _____

Author: _____

© 1993 Patricia S. Morris and Margaret A. Berry

FF - 19

Name_____ Section _____ Date _____

Character Traits

Select a character from the fantasy book you have read. Describe how you are like that character and how you are different. How would you like that character to change?

Name of Character _____ Description:	Your Name _____	
	Similarities to you	Differences from you
Appearance Strengths Weaknesses		
How would you change the book's character?	How would those changes affect the story?	

Title: _____

Author: _____

© 1993 Patricia S. Morris and Margaret A. Berry

| FF - 20 |

Name _____ Section _____ Date _____

Solving Problems As a Fantastical Being

After reading your fantasy, you are going to take on the *persona* of some fantastical being, perhaps a troll, a unicorn, a gnome, or some other being. Speaking in the first person point of view, write a letter to a governing body presenting your position on an everyday problem from today's world and how you might be employed to helping resolve it. Examples of problems include, but are not limited to: homelessness, pollution, crime, discrimination, military expenditures, taxes, education.

Identify the being: _____
_____
_____

Identify the importance of that being to the story you finished: _____
_____
_____

Identify today's problem:

List the suggestions:

Identify the governing body to which you will write: _____
_____
_____

On the back of this paper, write the letter.

Title: _____

Author: _____

© 1993 Patricia S. Morris and Margaret A. Berry

FF - 21

Name _____ Section _____ Date _____

The Meeting of the Beings

From two fantasy books which you have read, have the different fantastical creatures meet. Describe the two fantasy beings. Create a setting and a plot.

Fantastical Being #1: _____
   from story: _____
_____
_____

Fantastical Being #2: _____
   from story: _____
_____
_____

Where do they meet? _____
_____

Why? _____
_____

What happens?

Title: _____

Author: _____

© 1993 Patricia S. Morris and Margaret A. Berry

78

Name _____ Section _____ Date _____

FF - 22

What Purpose Does Fantasy Serve?

Judge the lessons learned from reading your fantasy book. Answering the following questions will help you evaluate. What were two or three of the lessons or morals? How did you react? How did they affect your life? List three basic challenges that were overcome in the book. Which of these challenges is most closely associated with your own life? What aspect of the manner in which the character overcame his problem would you use in dealing with problems in your own life?

Characters: _____

Setting: _____

Theme/lessons/morals: _____

_____

_____

How would you have reacted had you been the character in the story? _____

_____

How would this have affected your life? _____

_____

List three basic challenges that were overcome in the book. Put a star in front of the one which is most closely associated with your own life.

1. _____

2. _____

3. _____

In a well-written paragraph on the back of this paper, explain which aspect of the manner in which the character overcame his problem you would use in dealing with your own problems. (You may write a rough draft on scrap paper first.)

Title: _____

Author: _____

FF - 23

Name _____ Section _____ Date _____

The Path of the Hero

The life of the hero or heroine in your fantasy may follow a very familiar pattern. Briefly describe these events in the life of your hero/heroine. If the order as given here is not the same as in your book, number the order in which things happen.

Typical pattern: Your character: _____

Typical pattern	Your character
Obscure birth	
Signs of unusual talent at an early age	
First use of power, often causing problems	
A period of training	
Temptation(s)	
Contest(s) with evil	
Apotheosis (change into another form, perhaps death, usually in self-sacrifice)	

Title: _____

Author: _____

© 1993 Patricia S. Morris and Margaret A. Berry

FF - 24

Name _____ **Section** _____ **Date** _____

The Role of Clothing

After reading your fantasy fiction, evaluate the role of clothing by answering the following questions.

How are the major characters dressed?
   Name and describe:

   Name and describe:

How are the fantastical beings dressed?
   Name and describe:

Did you find any of the garb strange, not "going" with the story?

Identify any other use of clothing and how it influenced on the story.

Is there anything you would have changed?

Why?

Title: _____

Author: _____

81

FF - 25

Name_____ Section_____ Date_____

Has It Been Used Before?

List several items, creatures, and terms from the fantasy story that you finished. Research them in any of the reference books dealing with folklore or mythology, such as Funk and Wagnalls' *Standard Dictionary of Folklore, Mythology, and Legend*.

Item, creature, etc.			
Page # in story:			
Role in story:			
Background research:			
Difference between research and story:			

Title: _____

Author: _____

© 1993 Patricia S. Morris and Margaret A. Berry

FF - 26

Name _____ Section _____ Date _____

Create Your Own Fantasy Beings

After finishing your fantasy fiction and filling in **Activity FF–1**, put yourself in the middle of a fantasy. Are your fantastical beings little people who live behind a cinder block or larger-than-life characters who appear when you command? What problem in your life would be solved and how? What are your fantastical beings going to do when you no longer need them? You may continue your answers on the reverse of this paper.

Your new setting: _____

Your new fantastical beings: _____

Name and describe: _____
_____
_____
_____
_____

Their special habitat: _____
_____
_____
_____

Problems to be solved: _____
_____
_____

How? _____
_____
_____

What will happen to your fantasy creatures?

Title: _____

Author: _____

© 1993 Patricia S. Morris and Margaret A. Berry

Science Fiction and Fantasy Index

Symbols

2001: A Space Odyssey 12

A

Ab to Zogg: A Lexicon for Science Fiction and Fan 10
Adams, Douglas 3, 9
Adams, Richard 15
Adler, C. S. 26
ADVENTURE 3
Against Infinity 11
Aiken, Joan 15, 20, 23, 26, 27
The Air of Mars 5
Alan Mendelsohn, the Boy from Mars 3
Alas, Babylon 13
Alcock, Vivien 8, 27
Alexander, Lloyd 16, 18, 23, 25
Alice's Adventures In Wonderland and Through the L 25
ALIENS 3
Aliens in the Family 8
All in Good Time 14
The Amazing Power of Ashur Fine 29
Ames, Mildred 23
Anderson, Poul 9
ANIMALS 4, 15
Another Heaven, Another Earth. 7
Anywhere, Anywhen: Stories of Tomorrow 5
Arabel's Raven 15
Arkin, Alan 15
Armitage, Armitage, Fly Away Home 23
Arnason, Eleanor 10
Arthur, Ruth 18
Asimov, Isaac 5, 9, 11
Asimov, Janet 9
Asimov's Mysteries 5
An Atlas of Fantasy 24
Avi 21, 23

B

Babbitt, Natalie 24, 26
Bach, Richard 15
Bachman, Richard 12
Back to the Future, Part II 14
Baker, Betty 15
Baker, Margaret J. 23
Balyet 29
Banks, Lynne Reid 21
Barney and the UFO 3
Bartholomew, Barbara 27
Beagle, Peter 18, 30
Bear, Greg 3, 12
Beatty, Jerome 11
Bedard, Michael 23
The Beginning Place. 25
Behind the Attic Wall 24
Bell, Clare 4, 15
The Bell Tree 3
Bellairs, John 18, 21, 23, 27, 28
Beloved Benjamin is Waiting 20
Below the Root 25
Benford, Gregory 7, 11
Bestiary Mountain 8
Bethancourt, T. Ernesto 6, 26
Beyond Silence 20
A Billion for Boris 24
The Black Cauldron 25
Black Unicorn 30
Blackbeard's Ghost 30
Blackwood, Gary 7
Blossom Culp and the Sleep of Death 27
The Blue Hawk 22
The Blue Sword 23
Bond, Nancy 26
Bonham, Frank 9
The Book of the Dun Cow 16
Bosse, Malcolm J. 22
Boston, L. M. 18, 28
Bova, Ben 10
Bova, Benjamin 6
The Boy Apprenticed to an Enchanter 27
The Boy Who Reversed Himself 29
The Boy Who Saved Earth 14
The Boy Who Was Thrown Away 25
Bradbury, Ray 3, 10, 28
Breed to Come 5
Bright Shadow 23
Brin, David 7
Brittain, Bill 16, 28
Brock, Betty 15
Brooks, Terry 25
Building Blocks 8
Bujold, Louis McMaster 12
But We Are Not of the Earth 7
Butler, Beverly 18
Butterworth, Oliver 15

C

C.L.U.T.Z. and The Fizzion Formula 11
Caidin, Martin 11
Caldwell, Steven 12
Callen, Larry 15
Calling Earth 4
Cameron, Eleanor 12, 20
Captain Butcher's Body 18
Card, Orson Scott 8
Carlsen, Ruth Christopher 9
Carlson, Dale 9
Carroll, Lewis 25
Cassedy, Sylvia 24
The Cat Who Went to Heaven 15
Catwings Return 15
Cave Beyond Time 22
Central Park Underground 18
Chancy and the Grand Rascal 25
The Changeover 29
Charly 9
Chase, Mary 28
CHEMISTRY 16
Chetwin, Grace 29
Childhood's End 3
Children of Dune 17
Children of the Dust 13
Chrisman, Arthur Bowie 16
Christopher, John 10, 13
Church, Richard 18
Citizen of the Galaxy 12
Clark, Margaret Goff 3
Clarke, Arthur C. 3, 6, 12
Clarke, Pauline 21
Clement, Hal 11
Clifton, Mark 4
Coatsworth, Elizabeth Jane 15
Cobalt, Martin 18
Code of the Lifemaker 4
Cohen, Barbara 30
COLLECTION 16
COLLECTIONS 5
Collidescope 29
Colum, Padraic 27
COMMUNICATION 6
COMMUNITY 17
Conford, Ellen 28
Conjuring Summer In 23
Conklin, Groff 5
Coontz, Otto 28
Cooper, Louise 27
Corbett, Scott 16, 18
Coville, Bruce 4
Cresswell, Helen 17, 21, 26
Crichton, Michael 4, 7
Cross, Gilbert 22

The Cuckoo Tree 27
Curry, Jane Louise 14
Cyborg 11

D

Daley, Brian 3
Dalton, Annie 25
A Darker Magic 23
Day, David 24
The Days After Tomorrow 6
The Dead Zone 29
DEATH 18
Del Rey, Lester 7, 14
Delaney, Michael 16
Delint, Charles 25
Dereske, Jo 10
Devil's Donkey 28
DeWeese, Gene 4
The Diamond in the Window 30
Dickinson, Peter 6, 9, 22
Dickson, Gordon R. 10
The Dictionary of Imaginary Places 24
A Dictionary of Mythical Places 24
Diggers 17
Dirk Gently's Holistic Detective Agency 9
DISASTERS 6
The Discontented Ghost 18
Doctor to the Galaxy 9
The Dog Days of Arthur Cane 26
Dogsbody 4
The Doll House Murders 21
Dolphin Island 6
Donovan, John 15
Downer, Ann 28
Dozois, Gardner 10
Dragon of the Lost Sea 20
The Dragonbards 20
Dragondrums 19
DRAGONS 19–22
Dragons and Dreams 17
Dragon's Blood 20
Dragon's Milk 19
Dragonsinger 19
The Dreaming Place 25
Drowned Ammet 17
DuBois, William 22
The Dueling Machine 6
Dunbar, Robert E. 6
The Duplicate 8
Dupper 15
Dwarf Long-nose 28
The Dying Sun 7

E

The Earth Witch 29
Earthchild 9
Earthseed 13
Eddie's Blue-Winged Dragon 26
Emergence 13
Enchantress From the Stars 13
Encounter Near Venus 3
Ender's Game 8
Engdahl, Sylvia 5, 13
The Engineer of Beasts 5
The Enormous Egg 15
Enright, Elizabeth 26
Eon 12
ESP 6
Eva 9
EXPLORERS 7
Eyes in the Fishbowl 19
The Eyes of the Dragon 22
The Eyes of the Killer Robot 27

F

Fahrenheit 451 10
A Fall of Moondust 6
The Fallen Spaceman 4
False Face 29
FAMILIES 7, 20–22
Family: A Novel 15
The Fantastic Planet 12
Fantastic Voyage 9
Farmer in the Sky 13
Figgs and Phantoms 19
The Figure in the Shadows 18
A Fine and Private Place 18
Fisk, Nicholas 8
The Fledgling 15
Fleischman, Sid 25, 30
Fletcher, Susan 19
Fool's Run 11
Footsteps 20
The Forever Formula 9
The Forge of God 3
Forrester, John 8
The Fossil Snake 28
Foster, Alan Dean 14
Foundation and Earth 11
The Foundation Trilogy 5
The Foundling and Other Tales of Prydain 16
The Fox's Lair 11
Frank, Pat 13
Freaky Friday 21
The French Lieutenant: A Ghost Story 18
Friday 11

G

Galactic Warlord 12
A Game of Catch 21
GAMES AND TOYS 8, 21–22
Gardner, Craig Shaw 14
Garfield, Leon 18, 20, 30
The Gate of the World 22
GENETICS 8
Genie with The Light Blue Hair 28
Get Off the Unicorn 17
Ghost Cat 18
The Ghost Downstairs 30
The Ghost in the Noonday Sun 30
The Ghost Squad Flies Concorde 24
GHOSTS 18
Ghosts Beneath Our Feet 21
The Ghosts Who Went to School 19
Gilden, Mel 8
Ginsburg, Mirra 5
The Girl in the Grove 26
The Girl Who Owned a City 13
Goldclimbers 17
The Golden Serpent 16
Goudge, Elizabeth 20
Gray, Nicholas 16
The Great Gradepoint Mystery 27
Great Tales of Science Fiction 6
The Green Book 13
Green, Roger Lancelyn 5
Greenberg, Martin H. 5
The Griffin Legacy 22
A Griffon's Nest 14
The Guardian of Isis 9
Gulliver's Travels into Several Remote Nations of 29

H

The Hairy Horror Trick 16
The Halcyon Island 26
The Hallowe'en Tree 28
Hambly, Barbara 28
Hamilton, Virginia 20
Han Solo and the Lost Legacy 3
Harding, Lee 4
Harris, Christie 30
Harris, Rosemary 28
Harrison, Harry 5, 6
Hauff, Wilhelm 28
Haunted Island 19
The Haunting of Cassie Palmer 27
Hawdon, Robin 15
Heart of the Comet 7
Heart's Blood 20
Heartsease 6
Heinlein, Robert 10, 13

Heinlein, Robert A. 7, 11, 12
Herbert, Frank 17
The Hero and The Crown 27
Hildick, E. W. 24
Hill, Douglas 12, 23
The Hill Road 14
Hiller, B. B. 20
Hilton, James 30
HISTORICAL TIMES 9, 21–22
The Hitchhiker's Guide to the Galaxy 3
Hogan, James P. 4
Hook 25
Hoover, H. M. 3, 7
A House Full of Echoes 29
The House on Parchment Street 19
The House with a Clock in Its Walls 23
Hughes, Monica 8, 9
Hunter, Mollie 28

I

The Indian in the Cupboard 21
Instruments of Darkness 6
Interstellar Pig 8
Into Jupiter's World 6
Invitation to the Game 8
Isle of the Shapeshifters 28

J

Jackson, Shirley 17
Jason and the Money Tree 30
Johnson, Annabel and Edgar 13
Jonas McFee, A. T. P. 3
Jonas McFee, ATP 25
Jonathan Livingston Seagull 15
Jones, Diana 17, 23
Jones, Diana Wynn 4
A Journey to the Center of the Earth 12
Journeys of Frodo: An Atlas of J. R. R. Tolkien's 24
The Jungle Book 16
Jurassic Park 4
Just So Stories 16
Juster, Norton 29

K

Karl, Jean E. 7, 20
Katz, Welwyn 23, 29
Kay, Mara 29
Kelley, Leo P. 13
The Kestrel 18
Keyes, Daniel 9
KIDNAPPING 23–30

The King of the Golden River 27
King, Stephen 22, 29
  see also
    Richard Bachman
Kipling, Rudyard 16
Klaveness, Jan O'Donnell 22
Knee-Knock Rise 24
Knight, Damon 6
Knowles, Anne 26
Konrad 21
Kooiker, Leonie 23

L

Lady Hawke 22
The Lamp from the Warlock's Tomb 28
Langton, Jane 15, 24, 30
The Last Starfighter 14
The Last Unicorn 30
Lawrence, Louise 4, 13, 19, 25, 29
Le Guin, Ursula 15
Leach, Christopher 19
Leach, Maria 24
Lee, Tanith 30
LeGuin, Ursula 17, 23, 25
The Lemming Condition 15
L'Engle, Madeline 10, 14
Lesser, Milton 12
Let Me Hear You Whisper 16
Letters From Atlantis 29
Levin, Betty 14
Levitin, Sonia 30
Lightner, A. M. 9
Lindgren, Astrid 27
Linnets and Valerians 20
The Little Prince 27
Lively, Penelope 16, 19
The Lone Sentinel 10
The Long Walk 12
Lord of the Stars 7
Lord Valentine's Castle 14
Lost Horizon 30
Lost Threshold: A Novel 26
The Lottery 17
Lucas, George 3
Luenn, Nancy 17

M

MAGIC 23
The Magic Stone 23
The Magicians of Caprone 23
Mahy, Margaret 8, 29
Mainly in Moonlight 16
Makra Choria 27
The Man From P.I.G. and R.O.B.O.T. 5

Manguel, Alberto 24
Maria Looney and the Remarkable Robot 11
The Martian Chronicles 3
Master of Fiends 23
Matthew Looney's Voyage to the Earth 11
Mayhar, Ardath 27
Mayne, William 14
McCaffrey, Anne 17, 19, 20
McIntyre, Vonda 3, 7
McKillip, Patricia 19
McKillup, Patricia 26
McKinley, Robin 23, 27
McMahan, Ian 11
Me, Myself and I 14
Me Two 26
MEDICINE 9
A Memory of Dragons 13
Merriam, Eve 10
A Midsummer Tempest 9
Miss Ghost 18
The Missing Persons League 9
Mission to Mercury 7
Mister Corbett's Ghost 18
The Monster Garden 8
Monster Makers, Inc. 8
Moon of Mutiny 7
Moon of Three Rings 5
Moonwind 4
Mooser, Stephen 3
The Mortal Instruments 6
Mrs. Frisby and the Rats of NIMH 16
The Mummy, The Will, and The Crypt 18
Murphy, Shirley Rousseau 20
My Teacher is an Alien 4
My Trip to Alpha I 12
Myers, Walter Dean 16
MYSTERY 9, 24–30

N

Naylor, Phyllis 29
Nelson, O. T. 13
Nicholls, Peter 10
The Night Watchmen 26
Nightbirds on Nantucket 26
Nightmares From Space 4
Nixon, Joan Lowery 19
No Flying in the House 15
Noah's Castle 11
NONFICTION 10, 24–30
Norby and Yobo's Great Adventure 9
Norton, Andre 5, 27
Nostlinger, Christine 21
Not Your Average Joe 16

© 1993 Patricia S. Morris and Margaret A. Berry

Notes to a Science Fiction Writer 10
Nourse, Alan E. 7
Nova 4 6
Nutty Knows All 16

O

O'Brien, Robert C. 13, 16
Omega Station 11
The Omnibus of Science Fiction 5
On the Far Side of the Mirror 20
101 Science Fiction Stories 5
Orbit 9 6
Ormondroyd, Edward 9, 14
ORPHANS 24
OTHER WORLDS 25
Out of the Ordinary 25
Outer Space and All That Junk 8

P

Palmer, David R. 13
Palmer, Robin 24
Passey, Helen K. 19
Paton Walsh, Jill 13
A Pattern of Roses 19
Peck, Richard 27
PERSONAL CONFLICT 10, 26–30
Peyton, K. M. 19
The Phantom Tollbooth 29
The Pike River Phantom 24
Pinch 15
Pinkwater, Daniel 3
The Plant People 9
Pool of Swallows 18
Post, J. B. 24
Pratchett, Terry 17
Psi High and Others 7
Psion 7

R

A Rag, a Bone, and a Hank of Hair 8
Raskin, Ellen 19
Ratha and Thistle-Chaser 15
Ratha's Creature 4
Ray, N. L. 4
Red Wizard 21
The Reluctant God 22
The Return of the Twelve 21
Riddell, Ruth 29
The Riddle-Master of Hed 26
Ride a Wild Horse 9
A Ring of Endless Light 10
ROBOTICS 11, 27–30
Rocket Ship Galileo 7
Rodgers, Mary 21
Ronia, The Robber's Daughter 27

Rootabaga Stories 17
Rosalinda 19
ROYALTY 27–30
Rubinstein, Gillian 25
Ruskin, John 27
A Rustle in the Grass 15
Ryan, Mary C. 26

S

Saint-Exupery, Antoine de 27
The Sand Bird 23
Sandburg, Carl 17
Sanders, Scott Russell 5
Santesson, Hans Stefan 6
Sargent, Pamela 13
Sargent, Sarah 3, 25
Science Fiction Stars and Horror Heroes 10
The Science in Science Fiction 10
The Seal-Singing 28
Searching for Dragons 20
Secret in the Stlalakum Wild 30
The Secret Life of Hillary Thorne 26
Secret Under the Caribbean 10
Service, Pamela 22
Service, Pamela F. 4
Severn, David 26
The Shadow Guests 20
Shadow Witch 29
Shape Shifters 17
Shardik 15
Shen of the Sea: Chinese Stories 16
Siegel, Maxwell 18
The Silk and The Skin 26
Silverberg, Robert 6, 11, 14, 22, 29
Sing and Scatter Daisies 19
Singer, Isaac Bashevis 17
Singularity 21
Slater, Jim 14
The Slavery Ghosts 22
Sleator, William 8, 21, 29
The Sleep of Stone 27
Slote, Alfred 10, 11, 12
Smith, Stephanie 25
Snyder, Zilpha 19, 22, 25
Sobol, Donald J. 29
Something Upstairs 21
Song of the Gargoyle 22
Space Bugs: Earth Invasion 6
Space Demons 25
Space Raiders and the Planet of Doom 3
SPACE WAR 12
Space: 1999 - Alien Seed 12
Speak to the Rain 19
Spearling, Judith 19

The Spellkey 28
Sphere 7
Springer, Nancy 21
Stadium Beyond the Stars 12
Stahl, Ben 30
Standard Dictionary of Folklore, Mythology, and Le 24
Star Gold 13
Star Ka'at 5
Star Lord 25
Star Quest 12
Star Trek: The New Voyages 5
Star Trek: The Wrath of Khan 3
Star Wars 3
Starfarers 7
Starluck 14
Still River 11
A Stitch in Time 19
Stowaway to the Mushroom Planet 12
Strachey, Barbara 24
A Stranger Came Ashore 28
Stranger From the Depths 3
A Stranger in a Strange Land 10
A String in the Harp 26
Sudbury, Rodie 26
SUPERNATURAL 27–30
SURVIVAL 12
Sutton, Jean 7
Sweet Whispers, Brother Rush 20
Sweetwater 6
Swift, Jonathan 29
The Swing in the Summerhouse 24
The Sword in the Stone 24

T

Tatsinda 26
The Fellowship of the Ring 25
There Was This Man Running 4
The Third Magic 23
The 13 Clocks 27
Thirteen Uncanny Tales 5
Thorns 11
Those Who Haunt the Night 28
Thurber, James 27, 30
Time at the Top 9
The Time Machine 14
TIME TRAVEL 14, 29–30
A Tolkien Bestiary 24
Tolkien, J. R. R. 25
Tomorrow's Children 5
Tomorrow's Sphinx 4
Townsend, John 11
TREASURE 30
The Treasure of Green Knowe 18
The Trolley to Yesterday 21

The Trouble on Janus 10
Truckers 17
The Truth About Stone Hollow 19
Tubb, E. C. 12
Tuck Everlasting 26
Tunnel Through Time 14
Turner, Gerry 3
The Twenty-one Balloons 22

U

Under Alien Stars 4
UNICORNS 30
Unicorns in the Rain 30

V

Verne, Jules 12
Vinge, Joan 7, 22
Voight, Cynthia 8
The Voyage of QV 66 16

W

Wallin, Luke 22
Walters, Hugh 7
Wangerin, Walter 16
The War of the Worlds 4
The Warrior's Apprentice 12
Watership Down 15
Weaver, Tom 10
Webb, Sharon 9
Wells, H. G. 4, 14
Wheeler, Thomas 26
When They Came From Space 4
The White Dragon 20
The White Mountains 13
White, T. H. 24
Who Knew There'd be Ghosts? 28
Wibberly, Leonard 3
The Wicked Pigeon Ladies in the Garden 28
Wiessner, John 6
Wild Jack 10
Wilkes, Marilyn Z. 11
A Wind From Nowhere 16
The Wind in the Willows 15
The Wind's Twelve Quarters: Short Stories 17
The Winter of the Birds 17
The Wish Giver 16
Wismer, Donald 14
A Witch Across Time 22
The Witch Herself 29
The Wizard in the Tree 23
A Wizard of EarthSea 23
A Woman of the Iron People 10
The Wonderful O 30

Wood, Marcia 26
Wraiths of Time 27
Wrede, Patricia C. 20
Wright, Betty 21, 24
Wrightson, Patricia 29
A Wrinkle in Time 14
Writing Science Fiction and Fantasy 10

Y

Yep, Laurence 6, 8, 20
Yolen, Jane 17, 20

Z

Z for Zachariah 13
Zindel, Paul 16
Zlateh the Goat and Other Stories 17